The Solution

How Africans in America Achieve Unity, Justice and Repair

BY JAY MORRISON

2nd Edition
Published by: Good 2 Go Publishing
Typesetting: Mychea
Cover: Oddball Design

Jay Morrison
Founder & CEO
The Jay Morrison Brand
1170 Peachtree Street
Suite 1246
Atlanta, GA 30309
Office: 1-844-JOIN JMA
Fax: 1-888-847-5915
www.JayMorrison.net
ISBN # 9781943686575

Please note that much of this publication is based on personal experience and anecdotal evidence. Although the author and publisher have made every reasonable attempt to achieve complete accuracy of the content in this book, they assume no responsibility for errors or omissions. Also, you should use this information as you see fit, and at your own risk. Your particular situation may not be exactly suited to the examples illustrated here; in fact, it's likely that they won't be the same, and you should adjust your use of the information and recommendations accordingly.

Any trademarks, service marks, product names or named features are assumed to be the property of their respective owners, and are used only for reference. There is no implied endorsement if we use one of these terms.

DEDICATION

This book is dedicated to the mission and legacy of one of the greatest forefathers of the African people in America, Malcolm X, also known as El-Hajj Malik El Shabazz. Born May 19, 1925, assassinated February 21, 1965.

"We suffer from political oppression, economic exploitation and social degradation, all of them from the same enemy, the government has failed us, you can't deny that. Anytime you live in the 20th Century, 1964 and you're walking around singing "We Shall Overcome", the government has failed you."

(*Malcolm X - The Ballot or the Bullet*, 2006)

Same goes for living in the 21st Century, 2016 and having to still cry out, "Black Lives Matter". The government has failed us.

This solution hand guide is written intentionally for African people in America but should be observed by all races, nationalities and ethnicities to better understand the struggles, concerns and experiences of what our ancestors (Africans) went through and the challenges we still face current day. For the world to hold no one accountable for our near 300-year holocaust, our African enslavement and our non-repair after these blatant human rights violations is the biggest act of irresponsibility by man in modern times.

"The only way the problem can be solved, first the white man and the Black man have to be able to sit down at the same table. The white man has to feel free to speak his mind without hurting the feelings of that negro. And the so-called negro has to feel free to speak his mind without hurting the feelings of the white man. Then they can bring the issues that are under the rug out on top of the table and take an intelligent approach to get the problem solved."

"I for one will join in with anyone, no matter what color you are, as long as you want to change this miserable condition that exist on earth." – Malcolm X Oxford Union-London, England December 3, 1964, 3 months before his assassination (Little, 2014).

Malcolm X (center) born May 19, 1925 and assassinated in 1965 was a minister, human rights activist, and our forefather. He is identified as one of the most influential leaders in American history (Malcolm X, n.d.)

TABLE OF CONTENTS

What to expect from "The Solution" hand guide? 1
Preface 7
Fact Disclosure: The Wake Up 28
Capture and African Enslavement Era: 31
Jim Crow and Black Code Era: 39
War on Drugs & African Mass Incarceration Era: 52
The Solution - Unity & International Strategy: 69
The "Black Unity" Blueprint 75
The Need for Black Unity 75
Benefits to Black Unity 77
The Black Unity Strategy 78
Black Vote Day 80
The Vote 81
Pledge Allegiance To The African Flag 85
The Solution- National Strategy: 86
The Solution- Stimulation by Way of Education: 91
United Africans in America Repair Curriculum (UAARC)™ 96
Economic Repair 96
Moving OUR Community Forward! 96
The Solution- Stimulation by Way of Collaboration: 100
The Solution to Today's Biggest Socioeconomic Issue: Gentrification 106
The Solution- Stimulation by Way of Education: 111
United Africans in America 113
Repair Curriculum (UAARC)™ 113
Social Repair 113
Moving OUR Community Forward! 113
The Solution- Stimulation by Way of Elevation: 115
Conclusion 120
ABOUT THE AUTHOR 127
REFERENCES 129

What to expect from "The Solution" hand guide?

This hand guide is divided into three sections: Mindshift, Fact Disclosure, and Solution Action Steps. The purpose of this hand guide is to take our struggle past merely documenting our oppression, trauma and victimization suffered here in America, but providing real life, practical actions we as a people can take today to give ourselves Unity, Justice and Repair. I don't profess that this is the end-all be-all answer for Africans in America, however this will provide us a strong foundation and framework to build off of as we move forward into our better days.

Words You Should Know and Understand Before Reading:

There won't be many "fancy" words used throughout this Solution hand guide but there are a few words that I want us all to fully understand by definition. Feel free to reference this section as you read to fully grasp the full scope of the puzzle I am going to piece together for us.

Redress: Relief from wrong or injury; the setting right of what is wrong. Compensation or satisfaction for a wrong or injury.

- **Example:** Has there been any redress by America towards the Africans in America?

Enemy: Persons, nations, etc. that are hostile to one another. Something harmful or prejudicial (causing prejudice or disadvantage).

- **Example:** The American government has acted as an enemy of Africans in America.

  **This sounds harsh but by definition they have certainly been hostile towards our people for no apparent reason. We in turn have not been hostile back.*

Second Class Citizen: A person who is not accorded a fair share of respect, recognition, or consideration. A person whose rights and opportunities are treated as less important than those of other people in the same society.

- **Example:** In 2016, Africans in America are still second class citizens.

Colonialism: The control or governing influence of a nation over a dependent country, territory or people.

- **Example:** America practices colonialism in regards to its relationship with Africans in America.

Hate: To feel intense dislike, or extreme aversion (strong feeling of dislike, opposition, repugnance, antipathy), or hostility.

- **Example:** I hate knowing my people are still second class citizens as a whole, here in 21st century America.

Antipathy: An instinctive contrariety or opposition in feeling. A natural, basic or habitual repugnance, aversion.

- **Example:** There is a level of antipathy towards Africans in America ingrained in the government system that plays out through its policies and policing.

Oppression: The exercise of authority or power in a burdensome, cruel or unjust manner. The feeling of being heavily burdened, mentally or physically by troubles, adverse conditions or anxiety etc.

- **Example:** Living with the constant anxiety that your teenage son or daughter may get racially profiled, harassed or innocently arrested while driving home from school is a form of oppre-ssion.

Nationality: The status of belonging to a particular nation, whether it be by birth or naturalization.

- **Example:** Being black or African American is not a legal nationality, this is why Africans in Ame-rica have not been able to have a seat at the United Nations' World Court.

Denationalize: To deprive of a national status, attachments or characteristics. To deprive of national character or natio-nality.

- **Example:** America violated human rights cond-uct when it denationalized its African captives.

Genocide: The deliberate and systematic extermination of a national, racial, political or cultural group. The policy of deliberately killing a nationality or ethnic group.

- **Example:** The American government has perpetuated and participated in both the blatant and covert genocide of Africans in America.

Nationalism: Spirit or aspirations common to the whole of a nation. The desire for national advancement or political independence.

- **Example:** Marcus Garvey and Malcolm X both practiced and taught the philosophy of Black Nationalism.

Homogeneous: Composed of parts or elements that are all of the same kind, not heterogeneous (not of the same kind or type); of the same kind or nature, essentially alike.

- **Example:** Although Africans in America may have different countries of origin or tribal routes in Africa, it is quite obvious they are homogeneous in nature.

Nation State: A sovereign state inhabited by a relatively homogeneous group of people who share a feeling of common nationality.

- **Example:** If Africans in America were to one day unify, they would have a great chance to negotiate on a global level the opportunity to secure their own Nation State similar to the Native Americans who are a Domestic Dependent Nation.

Dual Citizenship: Also, called dual nationality. Status of a person who is a legal citizen of two or more countries.

- **Example:** If Africans in America were to unite and collectively become dual citizens of any supportive African nation, then that nation or country could represent Africans in America at the United Nations World Court. This is the only way Africans in America can hold the United States of America accountable for what the United Nations has called "racial terrorism" committed by the United Stated towards its African American citizens.

**All definitions retrieved from Dictionary.com*

PREFACE

It's very hard to be Black in America, and even harder to be Pro-Black a.k.a Pro-African or proud of your African heritage. There is some-thing about an African in America not being broken, not being submissive, but being in power, outspoken, free willed and independent that shakes the very core of this country's infrastructure, that tears at the seams of its fabric. So, in order not to ruffle any feathers many of us dumbed down our "Blackness", ignore the cries of our people in the ghettos, those left behind not as capable or fortunate as us and we assimilate to the culture of those who have been in control for the mere purpose of our own comfortability and convenience.

We call standing up or advocating for our people "active-ism" therefore only activists have to get involved, as if them being black and you being black isn't enough to warrant your participation. The main reason is because most of us are slaves to money and wealth and our incomes come from corporations who we feel will have an issue with our "Blackness", so even without a word they silence us and we in essence sell our people out. Even though other nationalities can parade their ethnic origins, you as an

African in America "know your place", you live under a microscope, not with full liberty as without consequence. If Jewish, Polish, Italian, Irish, Greek or Japanese people in America had your people's experience, do you think they would be as silent as you? Would their athletes and entertainers who have millions of dollars in disposable cash remain silent or just stick a toe in the fight every once in awhile, all for fear of corporate backlash for simply doing one’s humanitarian duty to his or her people? Don't you understand that that type of anxiety is abnormal and a form of oppression? We know it's not equal. We are truly second class citizens by definition and many of us are okay with it as long as we get the house with the picket fence or the latest Mercedes Benz. This is not the spirit of Malcolm X or the example of African pride, unity and love he left us with. Sometimes our celebrities or influencers will tiptoe the line and speak out in public but very seldom will they say in public what they would tell you or I behind closed doors or in the barbershops or in the hair salons. Even our activists hold back out of fear that their blatant honesty might cause them incarceration or an early, untimely demise. Our people know the truth but fear holds us back from speaking and living the truth, and this is why we are still oppressed today. Many of our most courageous and talented Kings and

Queens are silent in fear that they might be the next martyr of our freedom movement like Malcolm X or Dr. Martin Luther King. This is the greatest mistake of our race, to rather live as second class citizens than to risk dying for true freedom and equality. There is a part of the spirit of Malcolm that lives in me, I know this and profess it not to be the icon he was and still is but to merely be the truth teller that he was and hopefully half as courageous as he was. I don't fear death, if death is what it will take to set my people free, better yet, our people free, it is a small price.

"Once you change your philosophy, you change your thought pattern. Once you change your thought pattern, you change your attitude. Once you change your attitude, it changes your behavior pattern and then you go into some action!"

(Malcolm X - The Ballot or the Bullet, 2006)

INTRO: MINDSET SHIFT

In order for this solution hand guide to be effective, one must read it with a clear mind, a spirit of unity and without fear of the opinions or backlash of others outside of our community as African people in America. There will not be one racist or bias statement made or encouraged by me for I am not a racist or a bigot. I'm a God-fearing entrepreneur, father and humanitarian who just so happens to be African in America. I see it as my responsibility, my duty to help solve the unity, justice and repair issues that have gone unresolved since our existence here in America.

I know we have differences as African people in America and like our forefather, Malcolm X instructed in his 1964 speech "The Ballot or The Bullet" it's time we put our personal differences aside and focus on our commonalities and common objectives. Your religious beliefs are your personal beliefs, your civic organization affiliation is your personal choice or commitment, your skin tone or physical appearance is personal to you, your gender or sexual orientation is no business of mine, it is your personal business. I'm writing this hand guide to give us a blueprint to solve some long overdue nation business. I know some of the aforementioned statements has some of you enraged right now and that's because you're too stuck on the micro issues which causes you to lose sight of the macro issues, the larger concerns of our people - Unity, Justice and Repair. There's a saying, "don't trip over pennies on route to pick up dollars". We have to put the petty differences and our personal preferences to the side if this is ever going to work. I have no ego, no personal interest in leading a movement or starting another organization. My only goal is to contribute the God-given talents I have of critical thinking and strategic execution to our people's quest for Unity, Justice and Repair. It is my job, our job, to finish Malcolm's work and the work of all the many forefathers and foremothers who came before us. I don't care which leader you follow, what religion you are or are not, or what organization you participate in, as long as they are about Africans in America or Africans anywhere in the world taking our destiny into our own hands.

"Islam is my religion but I believe my religion is my personal business. It governs my personal life, my personal morals and my religious philosophy is personal between me and the God in whom I believe... Just as the religious philosophy of these others is personal between them and the God in whom

they believe. And this is the best way. Where if we could come out here and discuss religion we'd have differences from the out start and could never get together."

(*Malcolm X - The Ballot or the Bullet*, 2006)

I believe this holds true for all of our personal differences. Malcolm gave us the perfect example to follow in order to truly achieve unity. You have to put our larger objective over your personal beliefs. It's called being selfless. It is a small investment to make for the greatest ROI (Return On Investment) many of us may never see in our lifetime.

"Join any kind of organization, civic, religious, fraternal, political or otherwise that's based on uplifting the Black man and making him the master of his own community."

(*Malcolm X - The Ballot or the Bullet*, 2006)

I say the same of our Black women; our Queens are masters of not only our community but of the universe.

We must focus on us without being influenced by what others may think about our self-repair. We don't need the consent or approval of any other nationality or ethnic group to tend to our community business, just as they don't need ours or seek ours for their advancement and betterment. We have to break the habit of worrying about what others may think because we focus on our own unity, our own justice and our own repair. This does not make us racist or biased, this makes us wise and self-determined. Our people have had, and still have, a one-of-a-kind unique experience here in America and never unified as a nation of Africans here in America. We never received justice and still are fighting for it until this very day and we have never been repaired or have intentionally repaired ourselves collectively. It is our God-given right to do so, in fact it is our duty to do so and it is not something we should feel ashamed of or made to feel guilty about. It is ok for any culture, community or ethnic group to huddle up and take the necessary steps to preserve, restore and heal their people. The blueprint for how we do exactly this will be carefully illustrated in this Solution handbook.

Now, here's the most difficult part of our journey... Let's check our egos at the door! Right now. Please. For the sake of our people, all you have to do is don't let that little wicked voice enter your head that's going to make you think anything other than Black love, Black unity and Black repair. If it's creeping in and giving you doubt, giving you objection or arousing your ego, stop it now for the sake of our people. I come to you as a servant of our people, that means a servant to you as well, not as a dictator, messiah or leader. Let's please leave the gender, religious, financial and personal agendas in the closet. This solution hand guide can really work but not if you can't suppress your ego as a small sacrifice for the greater good of our people. Now is our chance.

"I don't think there's anything more destructive than two groups of Black people fighting each other."

(*Malcolm X: The Last Speech*- After The Firebombing, 2014)

I promise to make this very light and conversational, an easy read and straight to the point. I consider myself somewhat of an intellectual but I'm certainly no scholar. In fact, I dropped out of high school at age 16 and just barely graduated after taking the majority of my junior year off to take a crack at the illegal drug trade in a small town in New Jersey (Somerville). I was a runaway teen and homeless, four months after graduating high school I landed myself on Rikers Island, New York city's infamous county jail, facing 3 years to life in prison at 18 years old for a non-violent drug and handgun possession offense. That wouldn't be my last run in with the law, last felony or last prison stint. However, seven years later I was able to miraculously walk away from the streets and a young adult life of crime to become a pretty successful and influential real estate developer, celebrity realtor and entrepreneur. This book is not about me whatsoever but only what my life experiences and talents can lend to our solution having lived such a diverse life.

As Malcolm said, "If you've once been a criminal is no disgrace, to remain a criminal is the disgrace."

Now, in my late twenty's I had some economic awareness of the plight of African people in America (Black people) because of the nature of my involvement in real estate and my authoring my first book "Hip Hop 2 Homeowners: How WE Build Wealth In America", but had little to no social or political awareness or concern up until my awakening in 2014. As fate may have it, during a real estate conference in Las Vegas I ran into Anillia Wright who was one of the conference attendees where I was a guest presenter. During our lunch break Anillia approached me and asked if I could help use my "celebrity realtor" influence to help bring awareness to the suspected lynching of her brother Alfred Wright who was found dead, mutilated and naked in the woods in a rural town called Hemphill, Texas.

I immediately got chills because two nights before I had been surfing the TV channels at my condo in New Jersey and had stumbled on a news broadcast with Anderson Cooper of CNN showing the badly mutilated body of a black man in the woods; coincidentally this was Alfred Wright, Anillia's late brother.

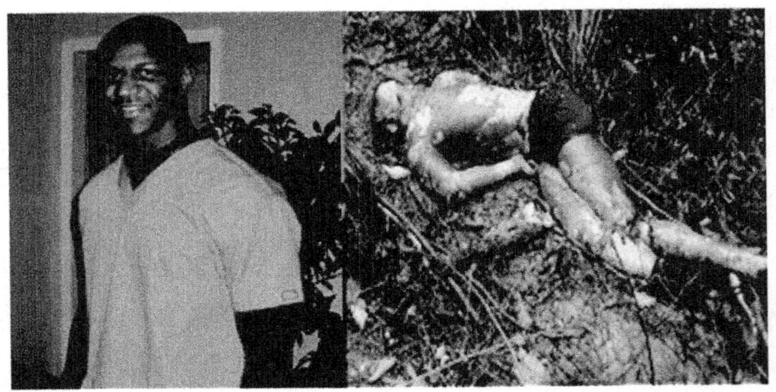

Alfred Wright (Levitt, R., & Feyerick, D., 2014)

So, I felt compelled to act, to get involved with a protest of injustice for the first time in my life at 33 years old. After our conference, I immediately flew to Texas and helped host a town hall in Jasper, Texas and also a protest in Hemphill, Texas at the sheriff's office. I had never felt so alive in my life. For the first time on a social or political level my life became larger than me and my personal goals. It became about the Wright family and justice for Alf-red. This would spiral me into a world of research and enlightenment on the true his-tory and experience of my people during our exist-

Jay Morrison (left), Activist, Quanell X (right)

ence here in America. During that first protest, I made friends with Sister Krystal Muhammad who was the acting chairwoman of the New Black Panther Party for Self Defense. She began to flood me with all of these facts, theories and philosophies about the condition of our people and strategies for repair. I instinctively thought she was crazy, just a radical, angry, militant black woman until I did my own independent research and found out that the depth of our history is so much deeper than what I learned in Adamsville Elementary School, Hillside Middle School or Bridgewater Raritan High School. For instance, right now there are many of you reading this who are frowned up that I befriended a "Black Panther", but let me ask you, how many injustices has the New Black Panther Party for Self Defense or the original Black Panther Party for Self Defense committed against our people? Here's an even better question, how many injustices has either Black Panther Party for Self Defense committed towards other ethnicities or innocent people? The same goes with the contempt many of you may have towards our forefather Malcolm X. How many innocent people has our forefather been responsible for harming, injuring or doing an injustice to? Often, we shy away or are ashamed of our own people who defended us and sacrificed their lives for us, but where did this feeling of contempt come from? Who made us feel they were bad people or taboo to be associated with? I agree that Malcolm and others may have said some really strong or even offensive things about other races of people as a whole, but we have to ask ourselves objectively, what environment or circumstances were they exposed to that would have them feel in such a way? How can we so strongly criticize someone's handling of second class citizenship and the blatant brutalizing and oppression of their people? Let's look at the root; if there was no racism, lynchings and government oppression, there would have been no resentment or counter aggression from the victims. It's quite simple; stop focusing on the "effect" and focus on what and who was the cause. Now, if I were to ask you how many injustices has the American Government been responsible for against our people, Africans in America, can you even count them? But

Jay Morrison (middle), Sister Krystal Muhammad (left), the late Alfred Wright's mother, First Lady, Rosalind Wright (right), in Jasper, TX)

yet you love America and are not ashamed of her. So, the organizations or leaders that have loved us through their actions, we hate or denounce but the organization and government infrastructure that has oppressed, brutalized and wronged us we love and pledge allegiance to. Interesting…

"As Afro-Americans or Black people here in the West-ern Hemisphere, you and I have to learn to weigh things for ourselves, no matter what "the man" says, you got to look into it."

(*Malcolm X: The Last Speech* After The Firebombing, 2014)

I know this is a strong way to start off this book but I cannot promise you'll like everything I say. I can promise you however, there will not be one single lie or misrepresentation in anything that you read today. You may not like it, because the truth often hurts. And the truth to a still colonized mind or brainwashed mind really hurts because it exposes your ignorance and blind trust, and exposes the games that have been played on us by a country that the majority of us have grown to love or have been taught to love since birth or ever since we could remember.

"I'm not the kind of person who's going to say what you like; I'm going to tell you the truth whether you like it or not."

(*Malcolm X - The Ballot or the Bullet*, 2006)

Back to my story, a few months after my partial awakening (I wasn't fully conscious yet), Sister Krystal invited me to a retreat they were having in a rural part of Mississippi, I reluctantly agreed. Two days before the trip I almost backed out once I found out there would be no cell phone access, modern hotels or decent restaurants. The thought of being in Mississippi for three days staying in double wide trailers with strangers didn't excite me in the least bit, but something in me told me to go. So, I went. I always listen to "something". During this trip, I had an amazing experience building with brothers and sisters from different parts of the country, food shopping together, cooking together, learning how to farm, practicing yoga, martial arts and even some hand gun trainings and target practice. One of my best two experiences of the entire trip was one night in a double wide trailer with two elders who quizzed me on my "blackness"... And I failed. I forgot the quiz questions, but trust me I failed miserably. Our elder bluntly put it to me, "Boy, you think white!"

Side note: Now I personally make a conscious effort to keep race out of our discussions except for that of our own race. I believe that we distract our focus and fuel unnecessary antagonization by pointing the finger at an entire race. Where we win is by focusing our efforts and finger pointing at ourselves (personal accountability) and at the government organization and structure that has historically and factually oppressed our people and still does till this very day. I believe in going for the guaranteed victory and that's what we are going to cover in this hand guide; our specific path to victory by way of Unity, Justice and Repair. I do acknowledge a system of European Supremacy or White Supremacy exists and this system is an infrastructure that must be dismantled, not a race of people. You can put Black people (as we know) in the system of white supremacy and the system is going to do what it was always created to do: leverage, disenfranchise and exploit Black people. So, let's focus on system bashing and not race bashing, for this will delay us from achieving our desired result. Remember, this is "The Solution".

So anyway, what our elder meant was that I was Americanized. I only had one way of thinking and he admittedly said he didn't blame me. I only knew that which I was taught. So, if a European American school system was the only education I had, then the majority of my points of view would be from the eyes or perspective of a European American i.e. a white person. This made all the sense in the world to me, so I began to intentionally see the world through the eyes of an African in America, not an African American. The view of America by the Indigenous Americans (Native Americans) I'm sure is a different view than the view they teach us in school. They don't see Christopher Columbus the same nor Thanksgiving or many other traditions or ideologies the descendants of European American settlers see as non-offensive or of no consequence. We as Africans in America have to see the world and our existence in America through the eyes of an African descendant or Black man or woman, not through the eyes of the people who controlled our ancestors or the government who still controls us till this day. But don't take my word for it, just ask our forefather Malcolm.

"There will come a time when Black People wake up and become intellectually independent enough to think for themselves as other humans are intellectually independent enough to think for themselves, then the Black man will think like a

Black man. And he will feel for other Black People and this new feeling and thinking will cause Black People to stick together and then at that point you'll have a situation where when you attack one Black man you are attacking all Black men. And this type of Black thinking will cause all Black people to stick together and this type of mentality will bring an end to the brutality inflicted on Black People."

(Malcolm X UC Berkeley Speech, 2014)

The second of my two greatest experiences on our Mississippi retreat was an accidental day with two really influential elders, Baba Joe (Joseph Epps- President of NCOBRA) and Brother Kamal. My first night with the previous mentioned elders opened my eyes to how I thought, viewed myself and the paradigm in which I viewed the world. This prepared me greatly for a 10-hour kitchen session with two lifelong freedom fighters and champions for our people. As fate would have it again, while everyone went to Jackson, Mississippi for a festival I got left behind and locked out of the main house due to a miscommunication of some sorts, so Bro. Kamal had to drive all the way from Jackson with Baba Joe to come let me in, or something like that. Nevertheless, my curious newly awakened mind was wide open and I wanted to know EVERYTHING. So, for ten hours straight I held both elders' hostage in the main house of a Mississippi ranch and asked every "why" question known to man. I needed to get to the root of why our people are in the state that we are in and how do we get out of it. I always go to the root and I always shoot for the solution. I never stay stuck at the problem. Quick story: On my last day of incarceration in New York prison in 1999, I was actually leaving a Work Release facility in Harlem, NY after serving the majority of my time in upstate New York cutting down trees for like 30 cents a day. As I'm walking down the stairs with my bag over my shoulder headed for the exit door to freedom, just like in a movie one of the older guys stops me and hands me a small piece of paper; it read, "there is no such thing as problems; only lack of solutions". This one quote changed my entire life. Since then I always look for the answers in everything no matter how dim the opportunity may seem. So later in this book I am going to lay out The Solution for Unity, Justice and Repair for Africans in America and African descendants throughout the world. I know that's a bold statement, yet I'm bold enough to say it and sharp enough to back it (all praises due to The Creator). This hand guide will show us step by step exactly what we can do to unify, exactly how we get justice and exactly how we begin to repair ourselves and secure the repair we are owed. I wholeheartedly believe in self-accountability for sure, but that doesn't excuse the accountability and redress that must be made by others, particularly the government of the United States of America. The great thing about this hand guide is I'm going to prove to you and to the world without a shadow of a doubt why America is accountable for current day condition of Africans in America and how it can be addressed fairly and enforced on a global level. I'm also going to hold my own people accountable and give us a blueprint for internal healing and repair for we cannot depend on others to do for us that which we can do for ourselves.

"If we keep it at civil rights, the only place we can turn for allies is within the democratic confines of America. But when you make it a human rights struggle it becomes international."

(*Malcolm X: The Last Speech*- After The Firebombing, 2014)

In 1963, a peaceful protester and black high school student, Walter Gadsden, being attacked by dogs (Selwyn-Holmes, 2010).

In this short hand guide, I am going to give everyone a very quick crash course on our history as we all should know it. Feel free to double check my facts and prove me right, I actually encourage it. The fact disclosure that I'm going to present next is going to be eye-opening for many of you who were like me in 2014 and only had a basic surface level education of the true experience of our people under this government. After reading these facts and examples from the three eras of our 397 years here in what is now known as the U.S.A, you will be awakened and ready to hear The Solution. But I must wake you up first!

I do want to acknowledge that research shows there was a population of darker skinned people or Africans here in modern day America before the arrival of the first African slave ships. We can divide ourselves into groups of those who were here first or who came in chains, but nevertheless our condition was the same and has been the same under one common government oppressor and we still share one common African lineage. So, let's not allow ideology divide us and detract us from the bigger picture of the experience of what the majority of our people suffered.

"One of the good parts about this racist system is it makes us all one."

(*Malcolm X: The Last Speech*- After The Firebombing, 2014)

Fact Disclosure: *The Wake Up*

For those of you who are overly patriotic Americans, reading this will offend you and you will instinctively want to defend America and say something insensitive like, "Get over it" or "Stop complaining".

This is your defense mechanism against the truth and what's special about this fact disclosure section is that it gives detailed historical facts all the way up to current day and shows how us Africans have been catching "hell" in this country before we even set foot on its land. Some of my fellow Africans who are lucky or more talented than others may turn their nose up and be happy with their own personal condition and use that or others who've had success like "the Black President of the United States of America", Barack Obama as proof this adverse treatment hasn't affected the whole of us. These same old tactics won't work, listen to our forefather Malcolm:

"They will deal with the condition but never the cause. They only gave us tokenism. Tokenism benefits only a few, it never benefits the masses and the masses are the ones who have the problem."

(*Malcolm X: The Last Speech*- After The Firebombing, 2014)

Also, what won't work is the blaming of ourselves for the condition we were put in. Blaming the victim is the most stupid rebuttal a person can make. And if you recall, several times in the intro to this hand guide I mentioned self-accountability, we will take ownership of our condition and improve it because not improving it only hurts us and satisfies our enemies. This does not negate, retract or excuse America for her crimes against humanity in relation to her treatment and non-redress of the African people in America.

"With skillful manipulation of the press, they're able to make the victim look like the criminal and the criminal look like the victim."

(*Malcolm X: The Last Speech*- After The Firebombing, 2014)

From the facts and historical examples below, you are going to gain four key things:

1. That the American Government has been intentionally negligent in its responsibility to repair the descendants of the Africans she so viciously demoralized, dehumanized and has committed genocide against.

2. That the physical, financial, mental, emotional and spiritual conditions of today's current Africans in America are a direct result of our lifelong experience in America during our entire 397-year history here, year for year.

3. That the realization of this is an acknowledgement that our condition is not our fault but the fault of the government that participated in our capture, colonization, dehumanization and demoralization without offering any redress, repair aide, restitution or reparation for its human rights violations of African people.

4. That based on the facts (not opinions), America has not been fair towards her African citizens. That we are second class by definition and there is still systemic oppression being carried out today and that every era fits together perfectly for the demise, destruction and devastation of the African in America.

Capture and African Enslavement Era:

(Factual Injustices Suffered by African People brought to America as Slaves 1619-1865, 246 years)

African slaves being transported for sale to African slave owners (African American Slaves, n.d.)

1. **South Carolina Slave Code 1712**

   African slaves were forbidden to leave the owner's property, unless accompanied by a white person, or obtaining permission. If an African slave leaves the owner's property without permission, "every white person" is required to chastise such African slave.

   - **Example**: For over 250 years elaborate systems of control were used to discipline rebellious sla-ves. The African slaves were proud, free and independent people in their native land. Law

Olmsted a famous Northern Architect provides a personal observation on how African slaves were treated. Constant punishment, chastisement, humiliation, torture and intimidation were some methods used. (Ladenburg, n.d.).

The garrote was a torture device used on African slaves. It would lock them into a seat with their back against a flat surface. Their neck was strapped with leather, string or a metal band, connected to a wheel or crank in the back. The wheel would turn so the African slave's neck was crushed slowly, eventually suffocating them to death. (10 Additional Gruesome Torture Devices, 2010)

2. South Carolina Slave Code 1712

Any African slave attempting to run away and leave the colony (later, state) receives the death penalty.

- **Example**: No African slave was permitted to leave the colony. "Masters forcibly paired "good breeders" to produce strong children they could sell at a high price. Resistance brought severe punishment, often death. (On the Masters' Sexual Abuse of Slaves: Selections from 19th- & 20th-c. Slave Narratives, n.d)

3. South Carolina Slave Code 1712

Any African slave who evades capture for 20 days or more is to be publicly whipped for the first offense; branded with the letter R on the right cheek for the second offense; and lose one ear if absent for thirty days for the third offense; and castrated for the fourth offense.

- **Example**: If caught, runaways faced certain punishment whipping, branding, castration and in many cases death. The most spectacular, and perhaps best-known, forms of resistance were organized, armed rebellions. Between 1691 and 1865, at least nine African slave revolts erupted in what would eventually become the United States. Nat Turner and several hundred comrades organized a revolt and the African slave owners killed over 100 enslaved were killed as retribution for the uprising and another sixteen African slaves and free blacks were hanged (Sweet, 2016).

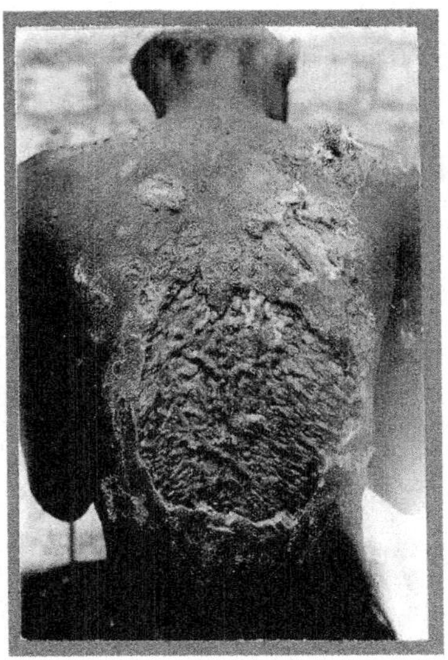

Wounds and scares on African slave, from being whipped by African slave owner. (African American Slaves, n.d.)

4. **South Carolina Slave Code 1712**

   African slave homes are to be searched every two weeks for weapons or stolen goods. Punishment for violations escalate to include loss of ear, branding, and nose-slitting, and for the fourth offense, death.

   - **Example**: Horrific punishments if caught stealing, including the cutting off of ears, and the pulling out of teeth, as well as the amputation of hands or death. (Turnbull, n.d.).

5. **South Carolina Slave Code 1712**

   No African slave shall be allowed to work for pay, or to plant corn, peas or rice; or to keep hogs, cattle, or horses; or to own or operate a boat; to buy or sell; or to wear clothes finer than 'Negro cloth'.

- **Example**: For African slave owners the rule is to never pay money for what can be made upon their estates, through African slavery. In other words, African slave owners expected enslaved people to perform a wide range of jobs that included cook, carpenter, boatman, cook, seamstress, and blacksmith, to mention only a few of the skilled jobs required around plantations, without ever providing financial compensation to the African slaves. Often working from sunrise to sunset over 10 hours per day, if in the plantation field. (Littlefield, 2016)

6. South Carolina Slave Code 1712

No African slave shall be taught to write, work on Sunday, or work more than 15 hours per day in Summer, and 14 hours in Winter.

- **Example**: The South Carolina Slave code prohibited African slaves from leaving their plantation, especially on Saturday nights, Sundays, and holidays. Slaves who violated this law would be subject to being whipped (South Carolina Slave Code, n.d.).

7. **South Carolina Slave Code 1712**

A fine of $100 and six months in prison are imposed for teaching an African slave to read and write, and death is the penalty for circulating incendiary literature.

- **Example:** "In the majority of southern states, if any person was caught teaching a slave to read the person teaching would be whipped, fined, or imprisoned. The slaves that were taught to read endured severe punishment of severe beatings to cutting off toes and fingers. Most slave owners felt that teaching these skills were not only useless, but dangerous. The rationale was that literacy would make the slaves more difficult to control and they could even start to run away." *("I will be heard!" Abolitionism in America, In Their Own Words: Slave Narratives, 2002).*

**Summary of all South Carolina Slave Codes derived from South Carolina Slave Laws Summary and Record (n.d.) and Wikipedia (*Treatment of slaves in the United States, n.d.)

8. **Virginia Slave Code 1862**

African slaves were prohibited from lifting a hand against a white person, even in self-defense. A runaway African slave refusing to surrender could be killed without penalty. (The Civil War in America: Slave Code for the District., n.d.)

- **Example**: "For many enslaved African Americans, one of the cruelest hardships they endured was sexual abuse by the slaveholders, overseers, and other white men and women whose power to dominate them was complete. Enslaved women were forced to submit to their masters' sexual advances, perhaps bearing children who would engender the rage of a master's wife, and from whom they might be separated forever as a result." (On the Masters' Sexual Abuse of Slaves: Selections from 19th- & 20th-c. Slave Narratives, n.d.)

9. **Virginia Slave Code 1705**

"If any slave resists his master correcting such a slave, and shall happen to be killed in such correction the master shall be free of all punishment as if such accident never happened."

(Virginia Slave Codes of 1705, n.d.)

- **Example**: "The slaves were the chattel of their owners to do with as they liked; really, except for speech, no different from a pig or a horse." (Permalink, 2012)

10. Louisiana Slave Code 1724

"The slave who, having struck his master, his mistress, or the husband of his mistress, or their children, shall have produced a bruise, or the shedding of blood in the face, shall suffer capital punishment." (Taylor, Q., Jr., n.d.)

- **Examples**: African slave women who resisted by raising their hands to their master, or any white person, were severely punished: if not by death, their hands would be amputated. (Turnbull, n.d.).

Jim Crow and Black Code Era:

(Factual Injustices Suffered by the African People during the Reconstruction & Jim Crow Eras, also known as the Black Code Era 1865-1965, 100 years)

1. The 13th Amendment

The 13th Amendment of the United States constitution was passed by the House of Representatives January 31,1865 and abolishes slavery but leaves a loophole where a party convicted of a crime could be enslaved or forced into involuntary servitude.

"Section 1. Neither slavery nor involuntary servitude, except as a punishment for crime whereof the party shall have been duly convicted, shall exist within the United States, or any place subject to their jurisdiction."

- **Example**: In a USAToday article Jim Liske identified that: "Half a century after the bombing, the struggle is not over, in part because language in that same amendment still undermines the equal humanity of more than 7 million Americans who have been convicted of a crime. Ratified at the end of the Civil War, the amendment abolished slavery, with one critical exception: Slavery and involuntary servitude actually remain lawful "as a punishment for crime whereof the party shall have been duly convicted." In other words, according to this so-called punishment clause, if you get pulled over with the wrong controlled substance in your trunk, there's nothing in the 13th Amendment to ensure you can't be considered a slave of the state." (Liske, 2014)

2. Black Codes

Laws created and passed in 1865 and 1866, immediately after the emancipation of the Africans to restrict their new freedom, subjugate the Africans to labor based low waged work or free labor based on false debts. Black Codes also restricted the rights of freed Africans to own businesses, buy and lease land, own firearms, move freely through public spaces and receive an adequate education.

- **Example**: During Jim Crow Blacks were given the worst jobs for the lowest pay. Certain good jobs were set aside for whites only. Workers of both races were stopped if they tried to form labor unions. Many blacks, and a few whites, were arrested and forced to work as African slaves in plantations and mines. (Brooker, n.d.)

3. Vagrancy Tactics

Vagrancy laws were included in the Black Codes which allowed government authorities to arrest Africans for not having a job, a job acknowledged by European Americans or for being homeless. When arrested, the freed Africans would be given a fine and court cost which they often couldn't pay and would be forced to work to pay off the debt of a European American who paid their debt in exchange for labor. Being that the Africans were new to freedom in America many had nowhere to live, no prior education, no employment or no savings whatsoever this became common practice and another form of continuing a version of African slave labor and involuntary servitude.

- **Example**: If vagrants ran away and then recaptured, they would be forced to work for no compensation while wearing chains and balls. This process was more formally known as the Act Providing for the Punishment of Vagrants.

This law came about shortly after the American Civil War. (Tarter, 2015).

4. Social Segregation

Jim Crow states passed statutes severely regulating social interactions between the races. Jim Crow signs were placed above water fountains, door entrances and exits, and in front of public facilities. There were separate hospitals for blacks and whites, separate prisons, separate public and private schools, separate churches, separate cemeteries, separate public restrooms, and separate public accommodations. In most instances, the black facilities were grossly inferior generally, older, less well-kept. In other cases, there were no black facilities no Colored public restroom, no public beach, no place to sit or eat.

- **Example:** A 1935 Oklahoma law prohibited blacks and whites from boating together. Boating implied social equality. In 1905, Georgia established separate parks for blacks and whites. In 1930, Birmingham, Alabama, made it illegal for blacks and whites to play checkers or dominoes together. *(Pilgram, 2000)*

5. Convict Leasing

Immediately after the 13th Amendment the practice of Convict Leasing began. Convict leasing is penal labor that forced those deemed guilty of a crime to be leased out to government, private businesses, firms or corporations who would have total control and responsibility for food, shelter and clothes of the prisoners. This was a legal way around African slavery that kept many freed Africans in the same forced labor conditions as slavery did. Convict Leasing became common practice from 1865-1928 and was continued in various forms until 1942 when it was abolished.

- **Example**: Southern state governments struggled to raise money to repair damaged infrastructure and to support new expenses, after the Civil War. Where and how to house, convicts became a problem. Many states paid private contractors to house and feed the prisoners and within a few years' states realized they could lease out their convicts to local planters or industrialists who would pay minimal rates for the workers and be responsible for their housing and feeding thus eliminating costs and increasing revenue.

Markets for convict laborers developed, with entrepreneurs buying and selling convict labor leases and unlike African slavery, employers had only a small capital investment in convict laborers, and little incentive to treat them well. (Blackmon, 2008)

6. Law Enforcement Discretion

Law enforcement discretion was widely practiced in where American police and courts could be selective on how harshly they punished freed Africans versus other citizens in America. The Africans were commonly accused of false crimes and targeted and cited for simple infractions that European Americans were not held liable for. This was often directed at the African men who were often taken away from their homes leaving their wives and children to provide for and protect themselves.

- **Example**: "Emmett Louis Till (July 25, 1941 – August 28, 1955) was an African-American teen-ager who was lynched in Mississippi at the age of 14. Till was from Chicago, Illinois, and visiting relatives in Money, a small town in the Mississippi Delta region. He spoke to 21-year-old Carolyn Bryant, the married proprietor of a small grocery store there. Several nights later, Bryant's husband Roy and his half-brother J. W. Milam went to Till's great-uncle's house and abducted the boy. They took him away and beat and mutilated him before shooting him and sinking his body in the Tallahatchie River. Three days later, Till's body was discovered and retrieved from the river." For her son's funeral, Mamie Till insisted that the casket containing his body be left open, because, in her words, "I wanted the world to see what they did to my baby." (Emmett Till, n.d.)

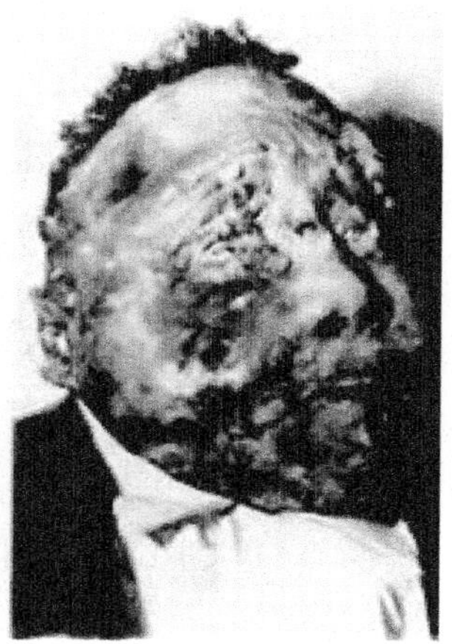

Mamie Till (left, mother of Emmett Till) and Emmett Louis Till in casket (picture on right). (Emmett Till, n.d.)

7. KKK and Lynchings

The KKK was formed and lynchings began to take place immediately after the emancipation of the Africans. Many vigilante groups such as the Ku Klux Klan were formed to preserve the dominance of white supremacy, to intimidate freed Africans and their supporters as well as to control the Africans' ability to vote, own land or have basic American liberties. These groups used a murderous tactic called lynchings which were comm-only killings by way of hanging, usually in public to instill fear and punish Africans they accused of crimes or infractions. Many KKK members were also law enforcement and government officials.

- **Example**: The Tuskegee Institute has compiled a list of lynchings by state and race from 1882 through 1968. According to Tuskegee, a total of 3,445 blacks were lynched during that portion of the Jim Crow era. Tuskegee's numbers are considered understated. (The Truth About Jim Crow, 2014)

When lynchings occurred, African slaves would often have a hook in their lung, attaching them to a tree, or hung while being set on fire, as depicted in this picture. (Ezeburio, 2015)

8. Jim Crow Laws

Jim Crow Laws mandated racial segregation of public schools, restaurants, water fountains, hospitals and almost all public facilities leaving the lesser functional and underfunded facilities to the Africans and providing more adequate facilities for European Americans. Jim Crow type of behaviors and segregation was also commonplace in banking, real estate practices, labor unions, health care, job hiring and would adversely affect the socioeconomic condition of the freed Africans in America. Africans were also limited in their ability to vote through loopholes in local laws and were withheld true equal representation for decades under Jim Crow and secretory practices. Jim Crow in the United States was enacted in 1890 and was mostly done away with by 1965 but continued in some instances until the early 1970's.

- **Example:** What the Fourth and Fifteenth Amendment gave, Jim Crow took away. The Fourteenth Amendment officially made African Americans citizens of the United States, making it illegal for any state to deprive any individual of life, liberty and property without due process of law. The Fifteenth Amendment changed all this. Almost all southern states passed statutes restricting suffrage in the years from 1871-1889. Various registration laws, such as poll taxes, were established in many Southern states. Over half the blacks who voted in Georgia and South Carolina in 1880 vanished from the polls in 1888. (Davis, 2004)

On May 28, 1963, a mob attacked college students and faculty members who opposed segregation by sitting at the whites-only counter at a Woolworth's five-and-dime store in Jackson. (Mississippi marks 50th anniversary of lunch counter sit-in that challenged segregation, 2013)

9. Redlining and Racial Steering

Africans were commonly denied loans or the opportunities to live where they desired but were strategically steered by banks, government agencies and real estate professionals into urban less desirable neighborhoods. Africans were also given mortgage loans with extremely higher interest rates and less desirable terms or were forced into private contracts with investors that had clauses in place to cheat them out of their homes even after satisfying their debt. This took place all over the country as Africans looked to cultivate farmland, own commercial properties or their personal residences.

- **Example:** "Segregation and poverty have created in the racial ghetto destructive environment totally unknown to most white Americans. What white Americans have never fully understood but what the Negro can never forget is that white society is deeply implicated in the ghetto. White institutions created it, white institutions maintain it, and white society condones it." (History Matters, n.d.; Washington: U.S. Government Printing Office, 1968)

10. COINTELPRO

Led by FBI Director J. Edgar Hoover, COINTELPRO was a FBI Counterintelligence Program which was used by the American government to discredit, disrupt, harass and dismantle Civil Rights groups and African leaders who sought to empower Africans and improve their conditions in America. Some of their tactics were as extreme as violence and assassination and as creative as media smear campaigns, wrongful imprisonment, planting false documents and creating internal friction amongst Civil Rights groups.

- **Example:** There is well documented evidence of Hoover and other FBI officials that referred to our national hero Dr. Martin Luther King Jr. as a liar, a threat, evil and some letters which made strong insinuations that he commits suicide. Hoover directed his agents to enact a heightened level of surveillance such as bugging, wiring, tapping and surveying Dr. King. (Weiner, 2012).

War on Drugs & African Mass Incarceration Era:
(Factual Injustices Suffered by the African People (commonly referred to as African Americans, Afro-Americans and Negroes) During the Post Jim Crow Era 1965-201, 50 years)

1. **Stop and Frisk**

   This program, instituted by the NYPD, empowers officers to stop & question pedestrians; this process is called "stop and frisk". Under the law, the officer is also allowed to frisk the civilian, if they presume the civilian has contraband or a weapon. From 2002-2015, 2.6 million black Americans have reportedly been subject to "stop and frisk" during police stops and street interrogations. (Stop and Frisk Campaign: About the Issue, n.d.)

   - **Example:** ***(NY Stop-and-Frisk of Young Black and Latino Men)*** "Young Black and Latino men were the targets of a hugely disproportionate number of stops. Though they account for only 4.7 percent of the city's population, black and Latino males between the ages of 14 and 24 accounted for 41.6 percent of stops in 2011. The number of stops of young black men exceeded the entire city population of young black men

(168,126 as compared to 158,406). 90% of young black and Latino men stopped were innocent." (Levine, 2012)

2. **The Enforcement Act of 1994 aka "The Three Strikes"**

This statute provides for mandatory life imprisonment if a convicted felon a) has been convicted in federal court of a "serious violent felony" and b) has two or more previous convictions in a federal or state courts, at least one of which is a "serious violent felony." The other may be a serious drug offense. (Ebenstein, 2014)

- **Example:** According to the ACLU, one in four young black men are under some form of criminal sanction, be it incarceration, probation or parole. Furthermore, in comparison to white offenders, a higher number of black offenders will be subject to life sentences because of prior drug offenses. (Ebenstein, 2014)

African in American men make up 37% of the American Prison Industrial Complex (America's New Slavery: Black Men in Prison, 2012)

3. The War on Drugs

The campaign was declared by President Richard Nixon in 1971 identifying drug abuse as "public enemy No. 1". Out of the "War on Drugs" came the DEA (Drug Enforcement Administration). There was also the public campaign "Say No to Drugs" started by the Reagan Administration, it used mass media campaigns, health studies, and public policies to dissuade drug use in America. (Timeline: America's War on Drugs, 2007)

- **Example:** The DEA trains police to conduct stops throughout the United States. Programs like *Operation Pipeline* launched in 1984. The federal program is administered by over 300 state and local law enforcement agencies it trains law enforcement to use pretext stops and consent searches on a large scale for drug interdiction. By the year 2000 the DEA had directly trained 25,000 officers in 48 states in Pipeline tactics. (Alexander, 2012)

Black women incarcerated during the African Mass Incarceration Era (Buckley, 2011).

4. Racial Profiling

Racial profiling by law enforcement is commonly defined as a practice that targets people for suspicion of crime based on their race, ethnicity, religion or national origin. Creating a profile about the kinds of people who commit certain types of crimes may lead officers to generalize about a particular group and act according to the generalization rather than specific behavior (Racial Profiling, 2013).

- **Example**: A massive police operation in Philadelphia that resulted in the helicopter bombing of the headquarters of a group known as MOVE. MOVE was a Philadelphia-based movement that focused on black liberation and a back-to-nature lifestyle. MOVE was founded by John Africa, and all members adopted the surname Africa. Despite two grand jury investigations and a commission finding that top officials were grossly negligent, no one from city government was criminally charged. (25 Years Ago: Philadelphia Police Bombs MOVE Headquarters Killing 11, Destroying 65 Homes, 2010).

The MOVE bombing, orchestrated by the Phildelphia massive police operation, killed five children, six adults and destroyed sixty-five homes. No charges filed, despite grossly negligent findings, per grand jury and commission reports. (25 Years Ago: Philadelphia Police Bombs MOVE Headquarters Killing 11, Destroying 65 Homes, 2010)

5. Plea Bargains

Plea Bargains can conclude a criminal case without a trial it is the result of a plea agreement between the prosecutor and defendant. In this agreement, the defendant agrees to plead guilty without a trial, and, in return, the prosecutor agrees to dismiss certain charges or make favorable sentence recommendations to the court. There are many documented cases that show defendants plead guilty to a lesser offense, an offense perhaps of a different category or one that they may not have actually committed (Plea Bargaining, n.d.).

- **Example:** Black Defendants were 19% more likely than whites to be offered plea deals that included jail or prison time. For non-misdemeanor marijuana cases, in particular blacks were 19% more likely to offered a plea deal that required time behind bars. This, according to data compiled from over 220,000 cases handled between 2010-2011 by the office of New York City DA Cyrus Vance (Demby, 2014)

In a New York Times article, Michelle Alexander noted that "...90% of criminal cases are never tried before a jury. Most people charged with crimes forfeit their constitutional rights and plead guilty" and this is especially prevalent in the African American community.

(Alexander, 2012, March 10)

6. Mandatory Minimum Statutes

Mandatory minimum penalties have been enacted over time for a variety of reasons. Foremost among these are legislators' professed belief that such penalties will bring greater certainty to the sentencing process and that they will "send a message" to potential offenders that specified behaviors will be met with harsh and certain punishment. Mandatory minimum penalties have not improved public safety but have exacerbated existing racial disparities within the criminal justice system.

- **Example:** African Americans comprise only 13% of the U.S. population and 14% of the monthly drug users, but are 37% of the people arrested for drug-related offenses in America. (11 Facts About Racial Discrimination, n.d.)

7. **Zero Tolerance Policies**

A "zero tolerance policy" is a school or district policy that mandates predetermined consequences or punishments for specific offenses that are intended to be applied regardless of the seriousness of the behavior, mitigating circumstances, or situational context. Several papers have documented the disproportionate representation of African Americans in school discipline and incarceration settings as a result of zero tolerance policies.

- **Example:** The Orleans Parish School Board's expulsions under zero tolerance policies were enforced 100% of the time on black students, with 67% of their school-related arrests being black students. The RSD-Algiers Charter School Association had 75% of their expelled students without educational services, all of which were black. Furthermore, 100% of their expulsions under zero tolerance policies and 100% of their school-related arrests were all black students (Discipline of Students without Disabilities, n.d.).

8. The School-to-Prison Pipeline

The policies and practices that are directly and indirectly pushing students out of school on a pathway to prison. Students are more likely to be retained, pushed out of school, are less likely to graduate and are more likely to get arrested or referred to the juvenile justice system.

- **Example:** A 2007 study by the Advancement Project and the Power U Center for Social Change says that for every 100 students who were suspended, 15 were Black, 7.9 were

American Indian, 6.8 were Latino and 4.8 were white. Furthermore, the U.S. spends almost $70 billion annually on incarceration, probation and parole. This number lends itself to a 127% funding increase for incarceration between 1987-2007. Compare that to a 21% increase in funding for higher education in the same 20-year span (Youth speak Out on the School-to-Prison Pipeline, n.d.)

9. Anti-Drug Abuse Act

Anti-Drug Abuse Act created distinctions in minimum sentencing between offenders who possess powder cocaine and those who possess crack cocaine. For crack cocaine, Congress departed from its "kingpin" and "mid-level dealer" categories and simply divided the amounts necessary for powder-cocaine sentences by 100. Thus 50 grams of crack, instead of 5,000 grams of powder cocaine, merit a ten-year minimum sentence, and 5 grams of crack, rather than 500 grams of powder, trigger a five-year sentence. Trafficking in 50 grams of powder cocaine carries no mandatory sentence.

- **Example:** In 2002, blacks constituted more than 80% of the people sentenced under the federal crack cocaine laws and served substantially more time in prison for drug offenses than did whites, despite that fact that more than 2/3 of crack cocaine users in the U.S. are white or Hispanic. (Criminal Justice Fact Sheet, n.d.)

10. **Voting Restrictions for Ex-Felons:** In the United States, an estimated 5.85 million adult citizens are currently disenfranchised as a result of a criminal conviction. While 15 states and the District of Columbia already restore voting rights upon release from prison, 35 states continue to restrict the voting rights of people who are no longer incarcerated. In 11 States, a conviction can result in lifetime disenfranchisement. Several States deny the right to vote to individuals convicted of certain misdemeanors (Reid, Cardin, Leahy, Durbin Lead Reintroduction of Bill to Create Nationwide Standard For Restoring Voting Rights For Americans Released From Prison, 2015)

    - **Example**: Felony disenfranchisement policies have a disproportionate impact on communities of color. Black Americans of voting age are four times more likely to lose their voting rights than the rest of the adult population, with one of every 13 black adults disenfranchised nationally. Of the 5.8 million Americans banned from voting 2.2 million of them are black citizens (Chung, n.d.).

Now that you've had this crash course in American History from the factual point of view of Africans in America, ask yourself these 5 Questions and Answer them honestly:

1. Has the American Government or its policing force acted violently or hostile towards Africans in America?

2. Has the American Government acted neglectful in its humanitarian duty to repair, restore, or award restitution for its denationalization, dehumanization, deculturalization and enslavement of African people in America?

3. Has the American Government given or supported the repair, restoration or restitution of other peoples in the world such as Indigenous Americans (Native Americans), Japanese Americans and German Jews?

4. Has the American Government participated in and or allowed bias policies, bias sentencing and bias policing of Africans in America?

5. Has the American government remedied the effects of the government redlining policy which created the climate for higher criminal activity by intentionally placing poorer, uneducated, disenfranchised people in close proximity of one another with limited resources?

I ask these questions because it makes the most patriotic "African American" in the world have to take an honest look at the true treatment his or her people have received under this regime. It also shows the direct link of injustice and oppression in every single era of our existence. Typically, our oppression is just minimized to African slavery and dismissed to being hundreds of years ago, when in fact our chattel enslavement just ended merely "two to three grandmas ago". These facts are indisputable and any person of any nationality should be enraged at how America has treated the African human beings she captured and kept under her authority. Imagine the same treatment you just read having happened to American Jews, Italian Americans or Korean Americans for the last 397 years. Would that be acceptable to you or them? No matter how you answer that, it is not acceptable to me, to us and this hand guide will finally give us practical action steps to remedy our oppression, the inhumane treatment and systematic genocide of our people.

"Any kind of act that is designed to delay or deprive you and me right now of getting full rights, that's the government that is responsible."

(*Malcolm X: The Last Speech*- After The Firebombing, 2014)

"My political, economic and social philosophy is Black Nationalism."

(*Malcolm X - The Ballot or the Bullet*, 2006)

The Solution

How Africans in America Achieve Unity, Justice and Repair

ONE

"We Suffer From Political Oppression..."

In this chapter I will provide real strategies for how we can end our political oppression both internationally and nationally. I will also lay out a very specific, detailed road map to how as a people we can receive long overdue justice by way of long overdue unity. Our unity is the foundation to everything we want to accomplish, everything we need to accomplish and everything we deserve. It is The Solution of ALL solutions.

The Solution - Unity & International Strategy:

"As long as you fight it on the local level of civil rights you're under Uncle Sam's jurisdiction, you're going to his court expecting him to correct you a problem. He created the problem, you don't take your case to the criminal, you take your criminal to court!"

(*Malcolm X - The Ballot or the Bullet*, 2006)

Our beloved forefather was so right. This was one of the most powerful strategies I learned back at that ranch house in Mississippi building with Baba Joe who coincidentally was the President of N'COBRA (The National Coalition for Black Reparations in America). During our accidental 10 hour building session I flat out asked Baba Joe, "If the Native Americans got status as a Domestic Dependent Nation, plus reparations in the form of land, tax advantages and financial restitution, and if the Japanese American descendants received restitution for just two years in American internment camps during World War 2, and if the German Jews received land and vast amounts of financial restitution and repair aid from Germany and America (who didn't even participate in their horrific holocaust), why not us? How has the world allowed America to completely neglect the repair, restoration, and restitution or reparation for African people in America?" And Baba Joe simply said, "Because according to the United States Supreme Court statues we have no standing in court because we are not technically or legally recognized as a nation of people or nationality." So, in short the U.S.A. has done it again, doping the African in America, beating us on a loophole although we know there's a preponderance of evidence and precedent already set with other nations of people they helped repair. But as always, no love for the Africans.

"When the government of South Africa began to trample on the human rights of the people of South Africa, they were taken to the U.N. When the government of Portugal began to trample on the rights of our brothers and sisters in Angola it was taken before the U.N..."

(*Malcolm X - The Ballot or the Bullet*, 2006)

However, the story doesn't end there! Me being the solution driven young King that I am I immediately fired back at Baba Joe and Brother Kamal, "Well, how do we become a nation?" And that's when things got interesting. Not only did I find out that there is a path to nationalization, I also found out it's not really that hard to do except getting a homogeneous, critical mass of people to all unite around one name, one flag, prove one like or common experience and common lineage or place of origin. For the majority of us, we know that's the continent of Africa although we arrived in America from an assortment of tribes and countries through the unfortunate experience called the Trans-Atlantic slave trade.

"...Instead you have to take that government to World Court and accuse it of genocide and all the other crimes it is guilty of today."

(*Malcolm X - The Ballot or the Bullet*, 2006)

The great part about this unity concept is that it's bigger than "reparations" or restitution. Pretend for a second that the opportunity for justice or redress didn't exist. Shouldn't we want to unify anyway? For the sheer sense of accomplishment, self-worth, self-pride, dignity and morale boost alone it's worth us living this out for our ancestors. Secondly, if we are to organize politically, boycott effectively or pool our resources economically this is a great way to identify who's in for our people and who's out. Let's draw the line in the sand today!

This one key element has stopped us from making significant progress. I'm not talking about starting another coalition, organization or 501c3 not for profit. I'm talking about establishing a legal national identity for ourselves and by ourselves for the first time in history. By doing this we then can control our own destiny as a people because we have first established who "we the people are".

I know this seems like a huge undertaking but I don't see it that way. I see it as logically necessary. We've already factually proven our oppression, factually proven our second-class citizenship and have factually stated the path to justice for these human rights violations. Nevertheless, please understand that we are the only nation of people in America outside of the Native Americans (Indigenous Americans) who have no home country of origin or nation to back them up. This forever puts us at a disadvantage, for there is no nation we are connected to whom America must be responsible to for its mistreatment of us, the African people. And unless you like being the disadvantaged, you need to take action and do something about it and this is exactly why our Creator has granted us this hand guide and blueprint at this specific time.

"This young generation doesn't want to hear anything about the odds are against us. What do we care about odds?"

(*Malcolm X - The Ballot or the Bullet*, 2006)

Many of us have extremely bright and well thought out ideas that could help move us forward but we have been missing this one key, very critical step- nationalization. We want to be respected as equals but we don't come to the table as equals. We as Africans in America have not yet until this day formalized our nationality in a civilized and sophisticated enough manner that we command the respect of America and other nations or nationalities of people. We operate as an informal group wanting formal results both nationally and internationally. So, here's how we do it...

The “Black Unity” Blueprint

#BlackVoteDay is a day of unity, activism, and self-determination.

The Need for Black Unity

The unification of Black people aka Africans in America is essential to our liberty, justice and repair.

Liberty can only be achieved once we are self-determined, civilized and sophisticated enough to take our destiny into our own hands despite the feelings, opinions and persuasion of others outside of our community. This happens through Black Unity.

Justice can only take place once we are a strong and organized unit that can effectively, strategically and collectively fight our oppressor. This too, only happens through Black Unity.

Repair must happen on two fronts in order to achieve full restoration within ourselves and our communities

1. There first must be ***accountability to ourselves and to our ancestors*** to rebuild our community's values, wealth, power and culture from within. This is our responsibility despite the oppression we face and non-repair of our people after our African enslavement, the black holocaust era, Jim Crow era and African Mass Incarceration era.

2. The second layer *of* ***accountability falls on the U.S. Government*** who has participated and benefitted from our oppression, chattel enslavement, mass incarceration and inhumane treatment for our entire existence on American soil, all while offering no repair aid, restitution or reparation to any generations of descendants and heirs of this horrific, traumatizing treatment. Black Unity is the only way to hold the U.S. Government accountable.

Benefits to Black Unity

Self-Accountability:

- Unification leads to effective organization against our oppressor: i.e. voting, boycotts, policy changes, self-governing, self-policing and self-protection.

- Unification provides a sense of self-worth, self-pride, dignity and an historic sense of accomplishment.

- Only a self-determined, unified Black people can take their destiny into their own hands and recreate their identity and culture. i.e. Adopting *our* own flag and pledge, honoring *our* foremothers and fore-fathers, establishing *our* own holidays, national anthem, deceleration, core values and repair curriculum for *our* people.

U.S. Government Accountability:

- Unification is the only path for legal nationalization and global recognition as a legitimate people with human rights protected by the World Court.

- Legal nationalization and global recognition are the only ways that Africans in America can hold the United States of America accountable for its 398 years of human rights violations against people of African descent in America i.e. denationalization, deculturalization, systemic racism, mass incarceration, chattel enslavement, enslavement by imprisonment, genocide, ethnic cleansing and systemic oppression with no repair, restitution or reparation granted.

The Black Unity Strategy

National Co-Chair of N'COBRA, Joseph Epps reported that the Supreme Court and United Nations World Court can ONLY issue reparations to a Nation of people. "African American" is not considered a legal nationality by either court and therefore "African American" people have no legal standing in Supreme or World Court. "African Americans" would have to take sophisticated steps to nationalization in order to be legally recognized as a people. The path to nationalization is as follows:

1. **Fact Disclosure-** Africans in America must make the world aware of our ongoing oppression and trauma

suffered at the hands of the United States of America and its racial terrorism of our people. This includes but is not limited to our status as only chattel property or second class citizens for our entire existence here in America. *(Reference the "The Solution" for your Fact Disclosure crash course.)*

2. **Plebiscite** - A plebiscite is a public direct vote by eligible voters to decide an important public question. Our public vote will be on our new legal identity (nationality) as our first step to finally unifying ourselves and legitimizing ourselves to the world.

3. **Decision & Declaration** - Africans in America must decide on a new name for our new nationality and decide on which African Nation we seek to petition for dual citizenship and openly declare our independence. This does not require that we quit our jobs, physically move, or forfeit our rights in America.

4. **Acknowledgement** - After our declaration of nationhood, we need only be recognized and adopted by one sovereign nation around the world who is a member of the United Nations World Court. This supporting sovereign nation can lobby our case to the world court which will allow us to have a seat as an observer at the world court and officially begin our path to respect and

independence and justice outstanding. Finally holding the American government accountable for its racial terrorism and human rights violations against the Africans enslaved in America and their heirs.

Black Vote Day

- A referendum of all African Americans to determine their identity, voting on how we desire to be identified as, signaling that our shared experiences, challenges, joys, hurts, and discrimination warrants us to be seen as a "nation within a nation;"
- Honoring our predecessors that have paved the road for the acknowledgment of our human rights as persons of African-descent, including El Hajj Malik Shabazz (formerly Malcolm X), and The Republic of New Afrika (RNA), Chokwe Lumumba, among others;
- A collective "Call for Restoration," demanding the respect and application of international human rights laws to address the generational systemic and societal racism inflicted on and experienced by persons of African descent here in the United States;

- During this United Nations International Decade For People of African Descent (2015-2024), a collective "focus-declaration" on policies (voted by the people) that we of African descent here in America will demand from elected officials, philanthropy, media, service providers (government and non-profit), and justice system.

The Vote

We organize the top 100 influencers in our community:

- 13 Religious Influencers
- 12 Business Leaders
- 25 Entertainers/Athletes
- 50 Social Activists

We organize an electronic or online voting system for the general public or partner with community groups for physical locations in major cities or townships.

Voting Power:

- 33% Religious Leaders, Business Leaders, Entertainers, and Athletes Vote

- 33% Social Activists Vote
- 34% General Public Collective Vote

Name Submission:

Submit 3-5 names for our new unified identity as a people. i.e. United Africans in America, Pan Africans, African Americans, New Africans etc.

The new unified identity with the most votes will be the new global identity of our people, determined by us. We can also vote on our flag, pledge, national anthem and other points of culture, on that date, allowing all to be involved in the creation of our new nation within a nation. These culture points can be submitted and promoted prior to Black Vote Day.

In our community, we have an identity crisis. This is why we cling to our religions, our organizations, our gangs, our different sides of town (east side vs. west side) etc. It's because we've been longing for some sense of identity. Well, now that opportunity is in our own hands to claim our national identity and be recognized by the world. This is something bigger than our religions (not bigger than our Creator but our religions), bigger than our fraternities, bigger than our gang colors, bigger than all of our affiliations or differences. Every nation in the world has a flag, every state in America has a flag, every city in every state in America has a flag, even every or most professional or collegiate sports teams have flags. Our name and our flag is essential to our identity, our unity and our quest for justice. The widely-accepted flag for our people is the Red, Black and Green (Black Liberation, Pan African or African Flag) given to us by our forefather Marcus Garvey.

Marcus Mosiah Garvey, Jr., ONH (17 August 1887 – 10 June 1940), was a Jamaican political leader, publisher, journalist, entrepreneur, and orator who founded the Universal Negro Improvement Association and African Communities League (UNIA-ACL), the Black Star Line, a shipping and passenger line which promoted the return of the African diaspora to their ancestral lands. (Marcus Garvey, n.d.)

I was spontaneously inspired recently to write a modern-day pledge to our flag that you can read below. As much as possible I like to always preserve our history and the vision of our forefathers and foremothers while still building on their visions for our current day fight in the 21st Century.

The root meaning of the Red, Black and Green in our flag is as follows: Red for the bloodshed of our people, Black for the people and Green for the land- Mother Africa. I accept these original interpretations completely, however in my pledge I did expound on these meanings in a forward moving direction. I bring this up because I respect our culture, our ancestors, our historians and our struggle. Had I not been awakened out of my sleep on an airplane on my way to Memphis, Tennessee when this pledge hit me, I would not think much of it. I'm not a poet or a pledge writer by any means but I do know God and our ancestors put something in my heart. If this is accepted or rejected by the community at large, so be it. There is nothing more important to me than our unity and there isn't anything I wouldn't sacrifice to see us under one flag, hand-in-hand in my lifetime God willing.

Pledge Allegiance To African Flag

**I pledge allegiance to the African flag
which represents Black Unity, Black Love
and Black Liberation**

**Black for the people in which I am proud to be a part,
Red for the love of my people with my entire heart
and Green for Black Liberation**

**Once and for all we will be free
spiritually, emotionally and economically**

Pledge Allegiance To The African Flag

I pledge allegiance to the African flag, which represents Black Unity, Black Love and Black Liberation. Black for the people in which I'm proud to be a part, Red for the love of my people with my entire heart, and Green for Black liberation. Once and for all we will be free spiritually, emotionally and economically.

The Solution- National Strategy:

"When I speak, I don't speak as a democrat I don't speak as a republican. I speak as a victim of Americanism called democracy."

(*Malcolm X - The Ballot or the Bullet*, 2006)

"We don't believe in voter registration, without voter education."

(*Malcolm X - The Ballot or the Bullet*, 2006)

I'm a big picture thinker and I'd rather focus on our bigger picture which is our international political agenda. However, I do understand that we are still living in America and need to find ways to make our experience here as fair as possible for our people as we simultaneously push our international agenda for justice and global recognition. The only way I believe we can accomplish this is by becoming more politically mature and more disciplined. We have to stop feeling like we have to vote for someone that we know does not have our community's interest at heart. Sometimes we might have to say "no" and don't vote if there is no one running who fits our criteria and lines up with our philosophy and ideologies. Let me tell you why. If I'm a businessman and I know you are going to spend money with me despite my lack of customer service or quality of product, all because you dislike my competitor more, I'll never give you what you really want or deserve because I see you as an undisciplined, immature, desperate costumer. You have no leverage. But if I knew in my heart that you would boycott me and be stubborn, be wise, be strong-willed enough to go without anyone's product and I realized it could cost me my job or me meeting company quotas, I then would bend and cater to your needs. We have to give ourselves leverage. If these politicians know we're simple enough to vote regardless of their lies to us, regardless of the oppression our people face daily, regardless of our unequal school systems, regardless of the incarceration disparity, then why would they respect us and why would anything ever change?

"Democrats have been in office eight years and what have we gotten out of it? We put them first and they put us last. We are political chumps!"

(*Malcolm X - The Ballot or the Bullet*, 2006)

"We must understand the politics of our community. And we must know what politics is supposed to produce. We must know what part politics plays in our lives. And until we become politically mature, we will always be misled, led astray, deceived or maneuvered into supporting someone politically who doesn't have the good of our community at heart"

(*Malcolm X - The Ballot or the Bullet*, 2006)

A second part of our national strategy must be to encourage able-bodied men and women within our community to infiltrate the political field with our interest and common agenda at the forefront. We must elevate them, endorse them and financially support them. We must also hold them honest and true to the promises they make to us and ensure they are not swayed by greed and power. This is easier to accomplish with the established legal, national identity of Africans in America.

"A political program of re-education to open our people's eyes makes us become more politically

conscious, politically mature and then when we get ready to cast our ballot, our ballot will be cast for a man of the community that has the good of the community at heart."

(*Malcolm X - The Ballot or the Bullet*, 2006)

I hope it is clear to you why we need to unify, who our common enemy or oppressor is (the American Government) and how we can position ourselves to have political power and to receive justice without begging, protesting or violence. We must simply do what civilized and sophisticated nations of people do and we will be respected as such. I know it sounds harsh to say that the American Government is our enemy or oppressor, but has her actions shown you otherwise? For all that we proved we have been through in our earlier fact disclosure, if America truly believed in justice she would be beating down our door to help heal us. Instead they focus on the oppression happening in other nations as if our cries, concerns and experience are not valid. That is not the actions of a government who respects the concerns of her citizens of African descent equally; by definition this is called second class citizenship.

We cannot be fearful any longer to speak the bold truth on behalf of our people.

"If you are scared to tell the truth you don't deserve freedom."

(*Malcolm X - The Ballot or the Bullet*, 2006)

"We have nothing to lose but our chains."

(*Malcolm X - The Ballot or the Bullet*, 2006)

"Our next move is to take the entire civil rights struggle into the United Nations. And let the world see that Uncle Sam is guilty of violating the human rights of 22 million Afro Americans and still has the nerve and audacity to stand up and represent himself as the leader of the free world."

(*Malcolm X - The Ballot or the Bullet*, 2006)

"We shall own, operate, and control the economy of our own community."

(*Malcolm X - The Ballot or the Bullet*, 2006)

TWO

"We Suffer From Economic Exploitation..."

This is true, we suffer from economic exploitation. We are exploited because of our financial ignorance due to the lack of financial education. Being exploited means we are taken advantage of economically by those who know more than us when it comes to money, banking, real estate, stocks, insurances, taxes, entrepreneurship etc. So, how we even the playing field is by being intentional and prioritizing the building up of our financial IQ. In this chapter we are going to cover ways in which we can teach ourselves on a mass scale and how we can collaborate to create more opportunities for our people. We must understand the spending power of our individual dollar and what that means to our community and our small businesses but also the power of our collective dollar and what kind of power that holds as a nation of unified African people in America on the same page.

The Solution- Stimulation by Way of Education:

"The economic philosophy of Black Nationalism only means that we have to become involved in a

program of re-education, to educate our people into the importance of knowing that when you spend your dollar out of the community in which you live, the community in which you spend your money becomes richer and richer. The community out of which you take your money becomes poorer and poorer."

(*Malcolm X - The Ballot or the Bullet*, 2006)

I often say that, "We don't know enough, about enough." This holds especially true when it comes to financial literacy and building family wealth. The masses of us have not been intentionally taught the strategies of wealth building, not even some of the most basic principles like homeownership, how to leverage credit or the importance of having a personal or family budget. When we increase our financial IQ and apply our new found financial intelligence to the philosophies of Black Nationalism and begin to intentionally spend our money as often as possible within our own community it will help create more jobs, more millionaires and more opportunities within our own community. This is simply a practice that we see applied every day in cities across America where other nationalities or cultural groups support their own community at every reasonable chance they get. It's why you see "Greek towns", "Little Italy's", "German towns", "Chinatowns", "Jewish or Hebrew sections" all over America. So, don't let anyone run the game on you that supporting our own is somehow racist or bias, especially considering we are in last place in the family wealth category in America, yet we spend the most money out of all "nationalities". So, if we spend the most, yet are still the poorest, this should tell you who's not getting our dollars. Us.

"And you and I are in a double trap because not only do we lose by taking our money somewhere else and spending it, when we try to spend it in our community we can't because we haven't had sense enough to set up stores or businesses in our community."

(*Malcolm X - The Ballot or the Bullet*, 2006)

It's amazing to see how accurate Malcolm's diagnosis are of our community some 50 years later. This is why a comprehensive financial education is so important for our economic success. We can all buy into the philosophy of "buying black" or "buying African" but if there are no businesses in our communities to buy from then it doesn't do us much good. Same goes for having established businesses in our community that aren't run properly, that don't provide quality customer service, that are under-funded, under-managed or are inefficient in some way. This makes it difficult for us to support our own. The only way we combat this is with education and collaboration. There is no shortcut to education, there are however creative ways we can leverage our talents and experiences to help pull each other up.

I have outlined a comprehensive economic repair curriculum that we all can share and utilize in our respective communities. The great part about it is, it's designed not to be labor intensive on any one person or organization but a blueprint to galvanize experts in different fields to lend their talents on a volunteer basis to the collective program so that our people can be exposed to the different areas of finance and economics they would most likely not be exposed to through traditional schooling. This program is called the UAARC or the United Africans in America Repair Curriculum. Feel free to build off of it and implement it in your local community along with the social repair side we will share later in this hand guide.

United Africans in America Repair Curriculum (UAARC)™ Economic Repair Moving OUR Community Forward!

What is the purpose of the United Africans in America Repair Curriculum (UAARC)?

The UAARC was created to serve as a blueprint for the repair of Africans in America socially, culturally, and economically.

How does the UAARC work?

Community partners such as educators, professionals, experts, and non-profit organizations will collectively volunteer to aid in implementing our 30 point UAARC curriculum in local schools, community centers, religious facilities, prisons, jails, residences, and areas of gathering.

Who can be an UAARC partner?

Community leaders, teachers, mentors, professionals, celebrities, activists, businesses, and social groups can all donate and volunteer their time, talents, services, locations, and resources.

Why is UAARC needed?

Africans in America are a nation of people who have suffered severe trauma, oppression, exploitation, and inhumane treatment during their 397 years in America without any intentional, comprehensive repair. UAARC aims to fill that void.

What will be accomplished within the community of Africans in America through the implementation of UAARC?

Africans in America will be empowered, educated, and exposed to a wealth of knowledge generally not accessible to them. Having access to such education and training will result in a more well-rounded, socially empowered and economically astute Africans in America.

United Africans in America Repair Curriculum (UAARC)
Economic Repair

United Africans in America Repair Curriculum (Economic Repair):

- Economic curriculum= 15 courses
- 1hr. for class; 30mins. for Q&A- 3 classes per week
  - ➢ 5 weeks of Economic repair overview

Economic Repair Curriculum
1. Introduction to Economic Stimulation & Financial Literacy 2. Credit Building, Restoration & Best Practices 3. Bankruptcy Strategies & Best Practices 4. Introduction to Real Estate & Homeownership 5. Real Estate Investing- Residential 6. Real Estate Investing- Commercial 7. Introduction to the Financial Market & Stock Trading 8. Introduction to Entrepreneurship & Business Formation 9. Advanced Entrepreneurship & Business Building 10. Personal Branding and Professional Etiquette 11. Job Training & Employment Readiness 12. Small Business Financing 13. Non-Profit Formation & Social Entrepreneurship 14. Business Franchising & System Creation 15. Alternative Businesses & Career Exposure

For those who seek higher level or more advance financial training please look into our repair scholarship we offer in my school, The Jay Morrison Academy. We also frequently offer free courses, books and learning opportunities outside of our tuition based courses. I try to remove any of my personal organizations from this repair conversation for fear of anyone wanting to link this Solution hand guide to any personal interest. I decided to briefly mention my school that I've worked so hard to build because it is what Marcus Garvey did in his books; he created schools and businesses for us and he gave us the opportunity to benefit from them, so did Malcolm from an organization standpoint. Nevertheless, I want to still recommend that no one enroll in any program of mine based on my word alone but please do your research, comparing and contrasting as you would with any other learning institution you sought to gain education from. I do not care where you gain your knowledge from, just by all means get it. Grow your financial IQ and build systems and institutions yourself to give it back. This is what we lack as a people, systems, curriculums and our own institutions. Now that we've identified this, let's be more intentional about solving this historic deficiency.

Whatever we don't have, we must create it ourselves or rely on those who have it.

I also want to stress the importance of mentorship in our community, this is one of the easiest ways we can help our people catch up. Each one teach some. That's right, we don't have the luxury for you to only mentor one person and spend the rest of your free hours enjoying life because you made it. We must be intentional about uplifting the whole of us. Just because you were first to escape, buy your freedom or read your way to freedom doesn't mean you neglect the rest of your people - not someone else's people, but your people. We must help ourselves. You don't need fancy classrooms or lecture halls to do this, take your message to our people in their schools, in their home, to their place of worship, to their corrections facility or even to their corner. The advancement of our people is solely on us and if you have knowledge or an expertise that they can benefit from it is your duty to give back. Think about the sacrifice that our forefathers and foremothers made for us before we were ever born. All because they wanted us to inherit a better life in America than they did. All we got is us.

"Anytime you have to rely on your enemy for a job, you're in bad shape."

(*Malcolm X - The Ballot or the Bullet*, 2006)

The Solution- Stimulation by Way of Collaboration:

One thing we have not effectively done historically as a community is pool our resources. We all talk about the nearly $1.3 trillion in spending power we are projected to have as a community yet we haven't been intentional enough, perhaps sophisticated enough or financially astute enough to leverage our buying power strategically for the good of our people. Because this is "The Solution", I am going to provide everyone with a solution template of one effective way my company is using to pool resources nationally and internationally for real estate development and acquisitions in our communities as a way to stop gentrification (a trend in urban neighborhoods, which results in increased property values and the displacement of low-income families and small business). I personally don't believe that "go-fund-me's" or donations to leaders are the most effective way for us to collaborate and pool our resources. I believe the people, our people, should have equity in whatever vehicle they park their money, thus giving them a vested interest in the success of the projects, initiatives or ideas, while allowing them to make a return on their investment and build family wealth. The model I am offering as a solution today will also address that age-old "transparency issue" where you only can donate or invest money blindly without knowing the status of your investment. I believe we have to elevate our people to be more financially savvy than that and allow them to participate and be in the know just as other nationalities would want to be in the know. We have to raise the bar for our leaders and demand more from them so they continue to grow and as leaders we must continuously challenge, elevate and stimulate our supporters and constituents. The smarter we all are and the more financially stable we all are, the stronger our community, the stronger our nation. I ask that no one take these solution offerings for granted or twist them and use them to the disadvantage of our people. I trust the integrity and good intent of each and every one of you as we live out wishes of our ancestors, creating a self-empowered, self-sustaining African community in America.

What I love about our model and what I love about real estate is that each transaction can create or stimulate as many as two dozen jobs (investor, various contractors, real estate agent, mortgage broker, title agent, attorney, inspector, insurance agent, property manager etc.). This is also how we beautify our own neighborhoods, make them safer and boost the morale of residents in the community. Real estate is the cornerstone of building wealth here in America, it is also the easiest business model to learn with a never-ending supply of customers and inventory (product - houses). The model I'm providing is how any of us can legitimately raise money or pool our resources while allowing the whole of us to benefit from the prosperity of our ventures.

This model can work for businesses or real estate development.

O.W. Gurley (left) and John B. Stratford (right) created the foundation of "Black Wall Street" in Tulsa, Oklahoma. "Black Wall Street" is known as one of the most prominent concentrations of Africans in America that owned businesses, in United States history (Greenwood Cultural Center, n.d.); Greenwood, Tulsa, n.d.).

The creation of Black Wall St. was intentional. In 1906 O.W. Gurley, a wealthy African moved to Tulsa and purchased over 40 acres of land. He only sold lots, homes and rented rooms to other Africans. John B. Stratford, was known for owning the luxurious 54-room Stratford hotel, fifteen rental houses and an apartment building. He believed that if Africans in America pooled their resources and spent within their community, they could become self-sufficient and ultimately achieve independence. Stratford's strategy proved to be so successful that he became the richest African man in Tulsa (Williams, 2014).

Pictures of Black Wall Street before the massacre and bombing of innocent Africans in America during the Tulsa Race Riot (Black Wall Street Images, n.d.).

In 1921, Black Wall Street was destroyed when Europeans murdered over 300 men, women and children who were residents of Black Wall Street. They also looted, burned, and bombed over 34 blocks of successful businesses and homes owned by mostly Africans in America (Black Wall Street Images, n.d.).

On May 31 and June 1, 1921, hundreds of whites led a racially motivated attack on the Black community of Greenwood in Tulsa, Oklahoma, killing some 300 people mostly Africans in America. The attack, destroyed more than 34 blocks of the district, then the wealthiest black community in the nation. More than 800 people were admitted to hospitals and more than 6,000 black residents were arrested and detained. The attack left an estimated 10,000 people homeless and destroyed 1,256 homes and 191 businesses. (Krehbiel, n.d.)

The Solution to Today's Biggest Socioeconomic Issue: Gentrification

What is the Tulsa Real Estate Fund?

TREF is a $50MM Regulation A Tier 2 fund that allows everyone to legally pool money to purchase real estate assets. Historically, prior to President Obama signing the JOBS act, the SEC prevented public involvement in funds such as ours. Now everyone can participate and benefit.

How Does It Work?

We, the Tulsa Management Team, will invest money in well vetted projects and jointly share profits with crowd investors. We will allocate an estimated preferred return of 8% to crowd investors. This means that before the Tulsa Management Team receives a dime in compensation, crowd investors will receive an 8% return first. Returns above 8%, crowd investors and management team will share profits 50/50.

Who Can Be Involved?

Anyone who is interested in investing into real estate can invest into the Tulsa Real Estate Fund.

What Are The Benefits?

- A Reasonable Performing Asset Class

  Crowd Investors have the opportunity to invest in a stable asset. The S&P 500 have returned 3.49% ROI from 1928-2015 while real estate has exploded past that number.

- Ownership

  Investors can own a piece of a large real estate asset that yields a reasonable ROI. At times the best real estate deals are enshrouded in scale and complexity. By investing as a collective, we have the opportunity to operate at a larger scale and be competitive as we compete for deals.

- "Investor First" Return Structure

  We believe that our investors come first. So much so, crowd investors received estimated preferred returns of 8%. On top of that, we are offering 50% of cash flow above the estimated preferred returns. With the S&P 500 ending -1% over 2015, we are providing reasonable returns with moderate to minimal risk.

- Socioeconomic Impact

  Some of our projects will be traditional real estate transactions. However, the vast majority will be community impacting projects focused on generating wealth in minority communities.

- Access to TREF Network

  Investors across the globe will become a part of the TREF network. This network will be encompassed of like-minded individuals. There will be multiple private events exclusively for shareholders. We also plan on having a yearly shareholders meeting.

  Together, we have the opportunity to control the future of our community.

  The figures and estimated preferred return reflected on this page are based on deal projections and are not guaranteed.

"And then what happens, the community in which you live becomes a slum, it becomes a ghetto, the conditions become rundown and then you have

the audacity to complain about poor housing and a rundown community. Why, you run it down yourself when you take your dollar out."

(*Malcolm X - The Ballot or the Bullet*, 2006)

"So, our people not only have to be re-educated to the importance of supporting Black business but the Black man himself has to be made aware of the importance of going into business. And once you and I go into business we own and operate at least the business in our community, what we will be doing is developing a situation wherein we will actually be able to create employment for the people in the community."

(*Malcolm X - The Ballot or the Bullet*, 2006)

"If you're Black you should be thinking Black, and if you're not thinking Black at this late date, well I'm sorry for you."

(*Malcolm X - The Ballot or the Bullet*, 2006)

THREE

"We Suffer From Social Degradation..."

What's wrong with that? A Black person thinking Black and not only thinking Black but thinking Black first. This is called social elevation. Think about it, you just read a brief overview of just a fraction of what our people have gone through for the last 397 years and counting, with NO repair or restitution. So, if no one else is thinking about us, is it wrong that we think about ourselves? Honestly, after our African enslavement, our holocaust, our trauma and proven second class citizenship what kind of person has an issue with us being intentional about healing, repairing and restoring ourselves even if we did get repair from some third party. Does anyone tell the Jewish community how they should function, or how their survivors should heal or repair themselves? So why do we have to answer to anyone? We don't. I'm providing you this argument because I know what kind of feedback you're getting from family, friends and maybe even coworkers. The fact that they feel that Black people, Africans in America, need their approval on how we handle our family business tells you in what view they see you as less than, subordinate and second class (and this goes for people of any nationality, even our own). We know what we've been through and what we're going through. We don't interfere with anyone else's business so they need to respect us as the equals that we are and stay out of our business unless they are rooting for us from next door or across the street. We have to shake that subliminal pressure society has placed on us every time we decide to stand tall, love ourselves, unify and seek justice. In this chapter, we will outline specific, practical, applicable solutions to cure our social degradation (the act of degrading).

The Solution- Stimulation by Way of Education:

"As long as you can be convinced you never did anything, you can never do anything."

There are so many social issues or deficiencies that our people face due to the severe trauma and inhumane treatment we've suffered. One of the biggest psychological warfare tactics that has been used on us is the intentional destruction of our culture, history, heroes and accomplishments. Not seeing or knowing about the many great accomplishments of our people prior to our capture and African enslavement era has put many of us in a box creatively and mentally. The anger, pain, resentment and effects of generational emasculation of our men and the degradation of our women has played heavily into our current day behaviors and warped culture. The breaking up of families during our African enslavement era and then mass incarceration of our men and women for over a century has broken up our homes and destroyed our parenting practices and family structure. All of this was done intentionally to break us, to keep us in a condition of poverty, distress and prone to criminal activity so this government can take advantage of the 13th Amendment loophole which still allows for African slavery if you're convicted of a crime. This is like some evil genius stuff. So, we know the problems and we also know I don't believe in problems, just lack of solutions. So, one solution I am granting our nation that we all can build on is the other half of our UAARC (United Africans in America Repair Curriculum). Again, this allows us to leverage our human capital to teach a comprehensive social repair curriculum to our people and allow them to get introduced to organizations or experts who can further help them where they have specific needs. Education is the key to our repair. Remember, they forbid us to be educated for a reason, now we have to play a major game of "catch up" and we have to be extremely intentional about it. Please make great use of our Social Repair Program in your community. I don't claim it, it is ours.

United Africans in America
Repair Curriculum (UAARC)™
Social Repair
Moving OUR Community Forward!

What is the purpose of the United Africans in America Repair Curriculum (UAARC)?

The UAARC was created to serve as a blueprint for the repair of Africans in America socially, culturally, and economically.

How does the UAARC work?

Community partners such as educators, professionals, experts, and non-profit organizations will collectively volunteer to aid in implementing our 30 point UAARC curriculum in local schools, community centers, religious facilities, prisons, jails, residences, and areas of gathering.

Who can be an UAARC partner?

Community leaders, teachers, mentors, professionals, celebrities, activists, businesses, and social groups can all donate and volunteer their time, talents, services, locations, and resources.

Why is UAARC needed?

Africans in America are a nation of people who have suffered severe trauma, oppression, exploitation, and inhumane treatment during their 397 years in America without any intentional, comprehensive repair. UAARC aims to fill that void.

What will be accomplished within the community of Africans in America through the implementation of UAARC?

Africans in America will be empowered, educated, and exposed to a wealth of knowledge generally not accessible to them. Having access to such education and training will result in a more well-rounded, socially empowered and economically astute Africans in America.

United Africans in America Repair Curriculum (UAARC)
Social Repair

United Africans in America Repair Curriculum (Social Repair):

- Social curriculum= 15 courses
- 1hr. for class; 30mins. for Q&A- 3 classes per week
    - ➢ 5 weeks of social repair overview

Social Repair Curriculum
1. Introduction to Social Repair 2. African History 3. Africans in America History 4. Spiritual Overview 5. New African Values 6. Anger Management 7. Conflict Resolution 8. Self-Defense 9. Parenting Counseling 10. Relationship Counseling 11. Health and Wellness 12. Self-Development 13. Ex-Offender/Citizen Re-Entry 14. Civil Law & Citizen Rights 15. Civil Disobedience & Social Change

The Solution- Stimulation by Way of Elevation:

"You can't hate your origin and not hate yourself. You can't have a positive attitude towards yourself and a negative attitude towards Africa at the same time."

(*Malcolm X - The Ballot or the Bullet*, 2006)

The biggest form of social elevation for Africans in America in my opinion is loving ourselves unconditionally! African love, Black love, African pride, Black pride and intentionally speaking life into one another. Because our culture was stripped from us and we have adopted a culture of self-degradation (degrading ourselves), we must reverse it and reverse it fast. We have allowed it to be okay on a mainstream level to call our women the worst kind of words and do it boldly and proudly. This is not our fault, we've been broken down to such low morale and character that we all have fallen victim. But to continue in this manner after what you know from our facts in this hand guide would be a total disgrace. What kind of people talk to each other with disrespect as the common language? Let's just change it, the power is in our hands, on our tongue. Let's make Malcolm proud! Let's uplift each other, uplift our women, haven't they had it hard enough? Let's uplift our fellow man, don't you think he needs to hear the positive reinforcement?

So, here's a suggestion that has worked well for me and many of my supporters. This is more of a matter of preference but I do want to challenge each reader to a 30 day challenge. What I have been doing to intentionally elevate our people in the simplest way (it costs you absolutely nothing), is the commitment of calling all of our women

Queens when greeting them, speaking to them or referring to them in any conversation including text or email communication. I have also made the commitment to do the same for all of our men, referring to them as Kings in every instance, even in a heated argument or debate. Now, I know you say "brother" or "sister" or "God" or whatever. Of course, you can disagree and we can trip over pennies trying to get our dollars, but what if, just what if we all said, "screw it, I'm in!". Imagine the vibrations and culture shift if every text you got said, "What's up King?" or "How you doing Queen?" And every rap song we heard replaced the N-word with King and the B-word with Queen? It would raise the entire self-esteem level of our people. Even for those that don't act like it, it would wear them down hearing the positivity all day. The same way if you call a positive-minded person "nigga" all day, he's bound to eventually act like a "nigga". There's power in words. That's why the African slave master and racist called us boy and girl or wench, because they knew the degradation would keep our heads down and spirits low. We've gotten so comfortable with it we even have our own slang now, we often call our Kings "King-King" and our Queens, "Boss Queen", there's nothing wrong with adding a little "flavor" to it. We are AfriCANS not AfriCANTS! Anything we want to accomplish is in our power. I know some macho King is saying, "I'm not calling no other man a King" and sadly the macho King was probably ok with calling him a "nigga". We've been programmed to hate ourselves so much it's like pulling teeth to love one another unconditionally (with no strings attached). Same for our Queens, you may not want to call another man King other than your significant other, well I say let him be your King and your brothers just be "King" or "King King". But again, this isn't law just merely a suggestion. As long as we unify under one flag I believe the rest will take care of itself. Our unity is our secret sauce.

Let me tell you a quick story before we close out this chapter. So, one night I was hanging out with a few Kings from Chicago and we were standing outside a local lounge when a Queen passed by. Now, whenever I see any human being I typically speak but I am extra intentional about making sure I speak every single time I see a fellow African because we need to start building a deeper bond and breaking the habit of being standoffish to one another. Remember, we are a family. This is what Malcolm was teaching us. So anyway, as Queen walked by I said, "How you doing Queen?" and she was shocked at first that I called her Queen, then she smiled and said she was doing well. So, one of the Kings I was with said to me, "You be killin em with that

Queen talk huh?" He went on to say, "You know, I know Black women who haven't been called nothing nice their whole life." So, what I said was this, "If you know Black women who haven't been called anything nice or positive their entire life then whose fault is that King?", "It's your fault!" "As a Black man that's your job! Who else you waiting for to uplift our women?" These aren't Asian women, European women, Russian women, they are our Queens and it's nobody else's foremost duty to uplift them than us, the Black man, the African man in America, "King King".

I'm not totally opposed to the terminology "Black" in reference to ourselves but we are more than a color. We are African people in America. Being Black won't get us accepted at the United Nations either. Nations respect nations, so I want to encourage us to get into the habit of referring to ourselves as Africans in America, United Africans in America. I didn't cover it here but we must start making international connections with our brothers and sisters of African descent all over the planet and connecting back to Africa, our homeland.

"You'd be surprised that deep within the sub-conscious of the Black man in this country, he's still more African than American."

(*Malcolm X: The Last Speech*- After The Firebombing, 2014)

Conclusion

"As you sow, so shall you reap. If you do wrong, you will get wrong in return. And if you do right you'll get right in return. When you're in another man's country, in another man's land, under another man's flag, under another man's government and under another man's court system, you'll have to look to that other man for justice and you'll never get it."

(*Malcolm X UC Berkeley Speech,* 2014)

I hope I have made a great case to wake up and put the majority of Africans in America into action. I know that there are many of you who are held down by your own personal interest and don't see the need to ruffle any feathers within your own life for the sake of bettering your people. I've proven the circumstance in which your people live in but because you are free and it doesn't affect you right now you have given yourself a pass, just like some house negroes or free negroes in our African enslavement era. They thought they were untouchable and a friend of the system until the system reminded them they were nothing but an African too. Don't be cowardly, don't be selfish, don't neglect your people because you got dealt a better hand or had the capacity to play a better hand. You never know when second class citizenship or oppression will strike home.

For those of you who are fired up and ready for action, I am with you not only in spirit but also in flesh for as long as The Creator shall have me here. I'm not a lecture-only kind of leader just good for speeches and panels, nor am I a social media blogger type of revolutionary. I am a front-line freedom fighter and truth teller. Please pay close attention to this next quote from Malcolm because it still applies today.

"When you start thinking for yourself, you frighten them. And then they try and block your getting to the public for fear that if the public listens to you, the public won't listen to them anymore. And then they've got certain negroes they have to keep blowing up in the paper to look like a negro leader

so that the people will continue to follow them no matter how many knocks you get on your head."

(*Malcolm X: The Last Speech*- After The Firebombing, 2014)

For many years, we have heard about the problems, the issues, the deficiencies in our community. Many of us wondered "Why are we so violent?" or "Why are we so socially immature?", "Why are we the most on drugs, the most in prison, the most single parent homes, the most high school dropouts?", "How did we get this way?". Well now you know exactly how and why. It is not our fault. This government intentionally left us in this condition and perpetuated a climate made for us to fail through its bias laws, bias policies, bias policing and bias sentencing. All because it has been hooked on the free and cheap labor of the Africans. We are the premier reason why this nation became one of the richest nations on this planet. And even for that she could give restitution and aid to those overseas who she has not inflicted but neglect her own injured citizens that she caused injury to.

If it's not plain to you by now what African people in America are up against, it may never be clear. Probably because you don't want it to be clear. There is no way anyone can argue you down on these facts; with the facts alone we win. But in order to win big we must unify.

However, we cannot get stuck on government accountability alone. We must roll our sleeves up and do the arduous work of repairing ourselves. This is where our people will begin to feel a sense of self-pride and dignity, when we pull ourselves up by the bootstraps despite not even having any boots and climb our way back into the dominant and independent people we once were. Marcus Garvey taught us that we were once the number one civilization in the world (this is historically true), we were the envy of all civilizations. And although we are in last place now just as others were in last place when we ran the world, we don't have to be in last place forever. But we must stop degrading ourselves, we must stop running from education and only concerning ourselves with entertainment. We must stop betraying our race, selling out, selling our soul for the material rewards of our oppressor. If you can't do it for you, for your babies or for me, then at least do it for Malcolm. Let's start comparing our love for our people to his love for our people, let's start comparing our sacrifice for our people to his sacrifice for our people. We have to snap out of this fog these people got us in. They want us ghetto, they want us coonin', they want us disrespecting our women, they want us high and drugged up and you know it. You feel it in your soul that something "ain't" right. But you, me, all of us have to be DISCIPLINED enough to make changes in our habits and behaviors to shake the strategic chains this oppressor has put on us. Just because they don't love us doesn't mean we shouldn't love ourselves. We have to love ourselves. Don't nobody else love us. We all we got.

Wake up.

"There will come a time when Black People wake up and become intellectually independent enough to think for themselves as other humans are intellectually independent enough to think for themselves, then the Black man will think like a Black man. And he will feel for other Black People and this new feeling and thinking will cause Black People to stick together and then at that point you'll have a situation where when you attack one Black man you are attacking all Black men. And this type of Black thinking will cause all Black people to stick

together and this type of mentality will bring an end to the brutality inflicted on Black People."

(*Malcolm X UC Berkeley Speech,* 2014)

ABOUT THE AUTHOR

Jay Morrison, also known as "Mr. Real Estate", is a successful real estate developer, celebrity realtor, author, TV personality, entrepreneur and social activist. Jay is the CEO and founder of the Jay Morrison Brand which is the parent company to Tulsa Real Estate Fund, a $50MM regulation A tier 2 real estate fund, Jay Morrison Real Estate Partners, a real estate consulting firm and the Jay Morrison Academy, an online real estate investor's school and mentorship program.

Despite being a high school dropout, an at risk youth and three time felon, Jay made a major life transformation for the better over a decade ago that not only made him a millionaire before the age of 30 but also propelled him into the national spotlight. He now uses his life experiences and personal story of triumph to empower and impact the lives of thousands of his Academy students, troubled youth, ex-offenders and real estate professionals throughout the world.

REFERENCES

African American Slaves. (n.d.). Retrieved March 17, 2017, from https://www.pinterest.com/shissa/african-american-slaves/

Alexander, M. (2010). *The New Jim Crow: Mass Incarceration in the Age of Colorblindness*. The New Press.

Alexander, M. (2012). Teaching the New Jim Crow. Retrieved August 31, 2016, from *http://www.tolerance.org/sites/default/files/general/The Lockdown.pdf*

Alexander, M. (2012, March 10). Go to Trial: Crash the Justice System. Lecture. Retrieved December 31, 2016, from *http://www.nytimes.com/2012/03/11/opinion/sunday/go-to-trial-crash-the-justice-system.html*

America's New Slavery: Black Men in Prison [Video file]. (2012, May 8). Retrieved May 19, 2017, from https://www.google.com/search?q=black men in prison slavery&espv=2&source=lnms&tbm=isch&sa=X&ved=0ahUKEwjH1sLYtKDTAhVh4IMKHdZqDR8Q_AUIBigB&biw=1366&bih=662#imgrc=3xD-jjx6AWYdgM:

Barnett, Ida Wells (1862-1931). (n.d.). Retrieved August 9, 2016, from *http://www.blackpast.org/aah/barnett-ida-wells-1862-1931*

Blackmon, D. (Director). (2008, March 25). *Slavery by Another Name* [Video file]. In *Public Broadcasting Service*. Retrieved August 31, 2016, from *http://www.pbs.org/tpt/slavery-by-another-name/themes/convict-leasing/*

Black Wall Street Images. (n.d.). Retrieved April 13, 2017, from https://www.google.com/search?q=black wall street pictures before the bombing&espv=2&source=lnms&tbm=isch&sa=X&ved=0ahUKEwjXsNPB3KLTAhUKcCYKHSCnC00Q_AUIBigB&biw=1366&bih=662#tbm=isch&q=successful black people in black wall street pictures before the bombing&imgrc=_

Brooker, R. (n.d.). The Five Pillars of Jim Crow. Retrieved August 9, 2016, from *www.http://abhmuseum.org/the-five-pillars-of-jim-crow/*

Buckley, A. (2011, December 12). I will not allow the beast to win! Retrieved March 19, 2017, from http://sfbayview.com/2011/12/i-will-not-allow-the-beast-to-win/

Burt, S. M. (2015, September 15). 10 key facts about the 16th Street Baptist church bombings. Retrieved August 9, 2016, from *http://www.nydailynews.com/news/national/10-key-facts-16th-street-baptist-church-bombings-article-1.2361565*
Chung, J. (n.d.). Felony Disenfranchisement: A Primer. Retrieved August 31, 2016, from

http://sentencingproject.org/wpcontent/uploads/2015/08/Felony-Disenfranchisement-Primer.pdf

Coates, T. (2015, October). The Black Family in the Age of Mass Incarceration. Retrieved from *http://www.theatlantic.com/magazine/archive/2015/10/the-black-family-in-the-age-of-mass-incarceration/403246/*
Davis, R. (2004, November 21). Creating Jim Crow: In Depth Essay. Retrieved August 31, 2016, from *http://voyager.dvc.edu/~mpowell/afam/creating2.pdf*

Demby, G. (2014, July 17). Study Reveals Worse Outcomes For Black And Latino Defendants. Retrieved August 31, 2016, from *http://www.npr.org/sections/codeswitch/2014/07/17/332075947/study-reveals-worse-outcomes-for-black-and-latino-defendants*

Discipline of Students without Disabilities. (n.d.). Retrieved August 31, 2016, from *https://assets.documentcloud.org/documents/562496/nola.pdf* Ebenstein, J. (2014, November 17).
For Some Convicted of Drug Offenses, the Punishment Never Ends. Retrieved from *https://www.aclu.org/blog/speakeasy/some-convicted-drug-offenses-punishment-never-ends*

11 Facts About Racial Discrimination. (n.d.). Retrieved August 9, 2016, from *https://www.dosomething.org/us/facts/11-facts-about-racial-discrimination*

Emmett Till. (n.d.). Retrieved August 10, 2016, from https://en.wikipedia.org/wiki/Emmett_Till

Ezeburio, P. (2015, October 29). 8 Most Horrific and Inhuman Black Slaves Punishment in The
History of Slavery. Retrieved September 12, 2016, from -http://answersafrica.com/8-most-horrific-and-inhuman-black-slaves-punishment-in-the-history-of-slavery.html

Emmett Till. (n.d.). Retrieved August 10, 2016, from *https://en.wikipedia.org/wiki/Emmett_Till*

Encarnacao, J. (2016, March 21). History's lesson: Ted Landsmark looks back at chilling moment in busing crises Retrieved September 12, 2016, from *http://www.bostonherald.com/news/local_coverage/unfiltered/2016/03/historys_lesson_ted_landsmark_looks_back_at_chilling_moment*

Ezeburio, P. (2015, October 29). 8 Most Horrific and Inhuman Black Slaves Punishment in The History of Slavery. Retrieved September 12, 2016, from *http://answersafrica.com/8-most-horrific-and-inhuman-black-slaves-punishment-in-the-history-of-slavery.html*

Greenwood Cultural Center. (n.d.). Retrieved April 13, 2017, from www.GreenwoodCulturalCenter.com

Greenwood, Tulsa. (n.d.). Retrieved April 13, 2017, from https://en.wikipedia.org/wiki/Greenwood,_Tulsa

History Matters: The U.S. Survey Course on The Web. (n.d.). Retrieved August 9, 2016, from http://historymatters.gmu.edu/d/6545/

"I will be heard!" Abolitionism in America, In Their Own Words: Slave Narratives. (2002). Retrieved August 10, 2016, from *http://rmc.library.cornell.edu/abolitionism/narratives.htm*

Krehbiel, R. (n.d.). The Questions that Remain. Retrieved September 11, 2016, from *http://m.tulsaworld.com/app/race-riot/timeline.html*

Ladenburg, T. (n.d.). Chapter 5: Methods of Controlling Slaves. Retrieved August 31, 2016, from *http://www.digitalhistory.uh.edu/teachers/lesson_plans/pdfs/unit45.pdf*

Lee, S. (Director). (2002). A Huey P. Newton Story [Motion picture]. U.S.: PBS.org.

Levine, H. (2012, May 9). Stop-and-Frisk 2011: NYCLU Briefing. Retrieved August 31, 2016, from *http://www.nyclu.org/files/publications/NYCLU_2011_Stop-and-Frisk_Report.pdf*

Levitt, R., & Feyerick, D. (2014, August 04). Texas man indicted in death of Alfred Wright. Retrieved September 13, 2016, from *http://www.cnn.com/2014/08/08/justice/mysterious-texas-death-indictment/*

Little, R. (2014, December 04). One of Malcolm X's final gospels. Retrieved September 12, 2016, from *http://www.oxfordtimes.co.uk/news/features/11646254.One_of_Malcolm_X_s_final_gospels/*

Littlefield, Daniel C. "The Varieties of Slave Labor." Freedom's Story. National Humanities Center. August 31, 2016. *http://nationalhumanitiescenter.org/tserve/freedom/1609-1865/essays/slavelabor.htm*

Liske, J. (2014, August 14). Yep, slavery is still legal. Retrieved August 31, 2016, from *http://www.usatoday.com/story/opinion/2014/08/14/slavery-legal-exception-prisoners-drugs-reform-column/14086227/*

Lundman, R., & Kaufman, R. (n.d.). Driving While Black: Effects of Race, Ethnicity, and Gender on Citizen Self-Reports of Traffic Stops and Police Actions. Retrieved August 31, 2016, from:*http://www.urbanaillinois.us/sites/default/files/attachments/04-social-science-subcommittee-report-part-1.pdf*

Malcolm X. (n.d.). Retrieved September 12, 2016, from *https://en.wikipedia.org/wiki/Malcolm_X*

Malcolm X - The Ballot or the Bullet [Video file]. (2006). U.S.: YouTube. Retrieved from *https://www.youtube.com/watch?v=CRNciryImqg*

Malcolm X: The Last Speech- After The Firebombing [Video file]. (2014). U.S. Retrieved from *https://www.youtube.com/watch?v=5deiqrP2tdA*

Malcolm X UC Berkeley Speech [Video file]. (2014). U.S. Retrieved from *https://www.youtube.com/watch?v=1W-EJAD8E30*

Marcus Garvey. (n.d.). Retrieved September 12, 2016, from

https://en.wikipedia.org/wiki/Marcus_Garvey#/media/File:Marcus_Garvey_1924-08-05.jpg

Mississippi marks 50th anniversary of lunch counter sit-in that challenged segregation. (2013,
May 27). Retrieved September 12, 2016, from
http://www.foxnews.com/us/2013/05/27/miss-marks-50th-anniversary-civil-rights-sit-in-that-challenged-segregated.html

Permalink, L. (2012, November 14). 1740 Slave Code of South Carolina. Retrieved August 31, 2016, from *http://www.duhaime.org/LawMuseum/LawArticle-1494/1740-Slave-Code-of-South-Carolina.aspx*
Pilgram, D. (2000, September). What was Jim Crow. Retrieved August 31, 2016, from *http://www.ferris.edu/jimcrow/what.htm*
Mississippi marks 50th anniversary of lunch counter sit-in that challenged segregation. (2013, May 27). Retrieved September 12, 2016, from
http://www.foxnews.com/us/2013/05/27/missmarks-50th-anniversary-civil-rights-sit-in-that-challenged segregated.html

On the Masters' Sexual Abuse of Slaves: Selections from 19th- & 20th-c. Slave Narratives. (n.d.). Lecture. Retrieved August 10, 2016, from *http://nationalhumanitiescenter.org/pds/maai/enslavement/text6/master/masterslavesexualabuse.pdf*

Plea Bargaining. (n.d.). Retrieved August 31, 2016, from *http://legal-dictionary.thefreedictionary.com/plea bargaining*

Racial Profiling. (2013, January 10). Retrieved August 31, 2016, from: *http://www.nij.gov/topics/law-enforcement/legitimacy/pages/racial-profiling.aspx*

Reid, Cardin, Leahy, Durbin Lead Reintroduction Of Bill To Create Nationwide Standard For Restoring Voting Rights For Americans Released From Prison. (2015, March 18). Retrieved August 31, 2016, from: *http://www.reid.senate.gov/press_releases/2015-18-03-reid-cardin-leahy-durbin-lead-reintroduction-of-bill-to-create-nationwide-standard-for-restoring-voting-rights-for-americans-released-from-prison#.V8hUADbr3cs*

Selwyn-Holmes, A. (2010, June 26). Iconic Photos: Birmingham. Lecture. Retrieved October 14, 2016, from: https://iconicphotos.wordpress.com/2010/06/26/birmingham/

Siemaszko,C. (2012, May 3). Birmingham erupted into chaos in 1963 as battle for civil rights exploded in South. Retrieved August 29, 2016, from
http://www.nydailynews.com/news/national/birmingham-erupted-chaos-1963-battle-civil-rights-exploded-south-article-1.1071793

Stop and Frisk Campaign: About the Issue. (n.d.). Retrieved August 9, 2016, from: *http://www.nyclu.org/issues/racial-justice/stop-and-frisk-practices*

South Carolina Slave Laws Summary and Record. (n.d.). Retrieved August 10, 2016, from: *https://canarypapers.wordpress.com/south-carolina-slave-laws-summary-and-record/*

South Carolina Slave Code. (n.d.). Retrieved August 31, 2016, from: *http://law.jrank.org/pages/11670/South-Carolina-Slave-Code.html*

Sweet, James H. "Slave Resistance." Freedom's Story. National Humanities Center. Retrieved August 31, 2016, from: *http://nationalhumanitiescenter.org/tserve/freedom/1609-1865/essays/slaveresist.htm*

Tarter, B. Vagrancy Act of 1866. (2015, August 25). In Encyclopedia Virginia. Retrieved from: *http://www.EncyclopediaVirginia.org/Vagrancy_Act_of_1866.*

Taylor, J. (1992). *Paved with Good Intentions: The Failure of Race Relations in Contemporary America.*
Taylor, Q., Jr. (n.d.). Louisiana's Code Noir (1724). Retrieved August 10, 2016, from Timeline: America's War on Drugs. (2007, April 2). Retrieved from: *http://www.npr.org/templates/story/story.php?storyId=9252490*

10 Additional Gruesome Torture Devices. (2010, July 18). Retrieved March 14, 2017, from: http://listverse.com/2010/07/18/10-additional-gruesome-torture-devices/

The Civil War in America: Slave Code for the District. (n.d.). Retrieved August 9, 2016, from: *https://www.loc.gov/exhibits/civil-war-in-america/april-1862-november-1862.html*

The Rise and Fall of Jim Crow [Video file]. (2002, October 1). Retrieved August 9, 2016, from: *http://www.pbs.org/wnet/jimcrow/*

The Truth About Jim Crow. (2014). Retrieved August 31, 2016, from *http://www.theacru.org/wordpress/wp-content/uploads/2014/07/ACRU-the-truth-about-jim-crow.pdf*

Treatment of slaves in the United States. (n.d.). Retrieved August 31, 2016, from: *https://en.wikipedia.org/wiki/Treatment_of_slaves_in_the_United_States*

Tulsa race riot. (n.d.). Retrieved August 9, 2016, from *https://en.wikipedia.org/wiki/Tulsa_race_riot*

Turnbull, H. (n.d.). Cannot Destroy My Spirit: Punishments Suffered By Slave Women. Retrieved August 31, 2016, from *http://scholar.library.miami.edu/slaves/womens_resistance/individual_essays/harmony.html*

United States. Kerner Commission, Report of the National Advisory Commission on Civil Disorders (Washington: U.S. Government Printing Office, 1968)
U.S. Public Health Service Syphilis Study at Tuskegee: The Tuskegee Timeline. (n.d.). August 9, 2016, from *http://www.cdc.gov/tuskegee/timeline.htm*

Vagrancy Act of 1866. (n.d.). Retrieved August 31, 2016, from: *http://www.encyclopediavirginia.org/Vagrancy_Act_of_1886*

Virginia Slave Codes of 1705. (n.d.). Retrieved August 10, 2016, from: *https://www.loc.gov/exhibits/civil-war-in-america/april-1862-november-1862.html*

Weiner, T. (2012, April 4). J. Edgar Hoover vs. Martin Luther King, Jr.: Book Exposes FBI's Targeting of the Civil Rights Leader. Retrieved from: *http://www.democracynow.org/2012/4/4/j_edgar_hoover_vs_martin_luther*

Williams, F. (2014, February 24). Black Wall Street: A Legacy of Success, Today's Black entrepreneurs expand upon the foundation paved by 1920s pioneers . Retrieved April 13, 2017, from: http://www.ebony.com/black-history/black-wall-street-a-legacy-of-success-798#axzz4eBAD7sFm

Youth speak Out on the School-to-Prison Pipeline. (n.d.). Retrieved August 31, 2016, from *http://b.3cdn.net/advancement/54c290ce86e7ee7c70_3d0m6ue80.pdf*

CPSIA information can be obtained
at www.ICGtesting.com
Printed in the USA
BVOW09s0100151117
500164BV00007B/55/P